Nicky Epstein's
Signature Scarves

Dazzling Designs to Knit

Nicky Epstein's
Signature Scarves

Dazzling Designs to Knit

Nicky Epstein Books

Nicky
Epstein
Books

An imprint of Sixth&Spring Books
161 Avenue of the Americas, New York, NY 10013
sixthandspringbooks.com

Editorial Director
ELAINE SILVERSTEIN

Book Division Manager
ERICA SMITH

Art Director
DIANE LAMPHRON

Associate Art Director
SHEENA T. PAUL

Yarn Editor
TANIS GRAY

Consulting Editor
ADINA KLEIN

Instructions Editors
EVE NG
CHARLOTTE PARRY

Bookings Manager
RACHAEL STEIN

Photography
JENNY ACHESON
ROSE CALLAHAN
JACK DEUTSCH STUDIO
MARCUS TULLIS

Illustrations
JANE FAY
SHIRI MOR

Copy Editor
KRISTINA SIGLER

Fashion Stylist
LAURA MAFFEO

Hair and Makeup
MARGRET AVERY

Vice President
TRISHA MALCOLM

Publisher
CARRIE KILMER

Production Manager
DAVID JOINNIDES

Creative Director
JOE VIOR

President
ART JOINNIDES

Chairman
JAY STEIN

Paperback edition
First printing 2014

Library of Congress Control Number: 2013033856

ISBN 978-1-936096-68-8

Manufactured in China

1 3 5 7 9 10 8 6 4 2

First paperback edition

sixth&spring
books

To my friend (sister,
    mother, advisor, critic,
thumbs-up movie critic,
    popcorn sharer, and
shopping companion)
Emily Brenner...it's my good
    fortune to know you!

58

53

44

38

14

126

10

88

64

132

112

Contents

When I was a little girl, my mother would wrap a handmade knitted scarf tightly around my neck to keep out the chill on a cold winter day. The scarf was practical, utilitarian and sometimes a little itchy.

Well, I'm a big girl now; and after traveling around the world and seeing how scarves are fashionably and fabulously worn by people of all cultures, I'm convinced that the scarf is one of the most important fashion accessories—one that can make or break an outfit.

Designing scarves is fun. Scarves offer an infinite variety of possibilities. They are chic, colorful, funky and fun and take a relatively short time to knit. Scarves say a good deal about the wearer's personality, and they make a great gift.

The signature scarves featured in this book use all kinds of materials, techniques and styles. I was fortunate enough to have one of my scarves appear on the cover of the 25th anniversary issue of *Vogue Knitting* magazine, and have included the instructions for the scarf in this book. Many of these designs really will keep you warm, but not quite like the heavyweight mufflers that your Aunt Becky used to send you at Christmas, bless her soul.

I invite you to make your favorites of these scarves, but I'm warning you—it can be addictive. Soon you may find yourself knitting a scarf for every one of your (or a loved one's) outfits.

I hope you have fun knitting these scarves.

Stay warm…be cool!

Nicky Epstein

 I'd love to hear from you!
Please visit www.nickyepstein.com

Majestic Fair Isle

Mixing a stitch pattern with a peerie and adding a flap edging gives a new twist to the classic Fair Isle look.

● **INTERMEDIATE**

SIZE
Approx 10" W x 60" L/25.5cm x 152.5cm excluding fringe

NOTE
Scarf is knitted in the round, creating a double thickness.

STITCH GLOSSARY
LT K the 2nd st on LH needle, k the first st on LH needle, slip both sts from needle tog.

TEXTURE PATTERN
Rnds 1 and 2 Knit.
Rnd 3 *LT, p2; rep from * around.
Rnd 4 *K2, p2; rep from * around.
Rep rnds 1– 4 for texture pat.

SCARF
With A, cast on 96 sts. Place marker for end of rnd and join. K 2 rnds.
Beg Fair Isle Pat
Work rnds 1–39 of Fair Isle chart twice, then work rnds 1 to 3 once more.
Beg Texture Pat
*Rep rnds 1–4 of Texture pat 6 times, then work rnds 1–3 of Fair Isle chart; rep from * 5 times more.
Beg Fair Isle Pat
Then work rnds 39–1 of Fair Isle chart twice. Change to A and k 2 rnds. Bind off.

MATERIALS
● 4 1¾oz/50g skeins (each approx 109yd/100m) of Cascade Yarns *Dolce* (alpaca/silk/wool) in #941 dark brown (A)

● 1 each in #973 turquoise (B), #916 olive (C), #912 tan (D), #927 teal (E), #955 orange (F), #940 beige (G), #924 rust (H), #958 sea green (I)

● Size 8 (5mm) circular needle, 16"/40cm long

● Stitch marker

● 2 purchased clasps

GAUGES
20 sts and 22 rnds = 4"/10cm over Fair Isle pat

22 sts and 24 rnds = 4"/10cm over Texture pat

The **crown motif** *is key here.*
Have fun and **find a closure** *of your choice.*

COLOR KEY

☐ Dk brown #941 (A)
▨ Turquoise #973 (B)
▨ Olive #916 (C)
▨ Tan #912 (D)
▨ Teal #927 (E)
▨ Orange #955 (F)
ᐯ Beige #940 (G)
▨ Rust #924 (H)
ᐯ Sea green #958 (I)

The chart rows are numbered 1, 10, 20, 30, 39. The bottom of the chart is labeled **12-st rep**.

FINISHING

Weave in ends. Sew both ends of scarf closed. Sew clasps to center front of scarf, see photo.

FRINGE

(make 2)
Cast on 6 sts.
Row 1 *K1, p1; rep from * to end.
Row 2 *P1, k1; rep from * to end.
Rep rows 1 and 2 for 7"/18cm.
Break yarn. With same needle, cast on 6 sts and work another flap. Cont in this manner until 4 flaps are on needle.

JOIN FLAPS

Row 1 (RS) *Work 6 sts from 1 flap on LH needle, lift other end of flap, twist, then pick up and k 6 sts across WS of cast-on edge; rep from * to end.
Row 2 Work in seed st.
Bind off.
Sew a fringe to each end of scarf. ☙

Patchwork Floral

To make the flowers,
I took a pattern for
a knitted edging and
gave it a spin!

MATERIALS

- 1 1¾oz/50g skein
(each approx 110yd/100m) of
Alchemy Yarns of
Transformation *Synchronicity*
(wool/silk) each in #98C
mediterranean (A), #91M
copper (B), #13A raspberry
crush (C), #82W janboy's
sapphire (D) #71F richberry (E)

- Size 6 (4mm) needles

GAUGE

22 sts and 30 rows =
4"/10cm over St st

● **VERY EASY**

SIZE
Approx 6" W x 58" L/15cm x 147cm

SCARF
With A, cast on 27 sts. Work 40 rows
in St st, beg with a k row.
Next row (RS) Change to B and k 1 row,
then work 40 rows in reverse St st.
Next row (WS) Change to C, and p 1
row, then work 40 rows in St st.
Next row (RS) Change to D and k 1 row,
then work 40 rows in reverse St st.
Next row (WS) Change to E and p 1 row,
then work 40 rows in St st.
Next row (RS) Change to A and k 1 row,
then work 40 rows in reverse St st.
Next row (WS) Change to B and p 1 row,
then work 40 rows in St st.
Next row (RS) Change to C and k 1 row,
then work 40 rows in reverse St st.
Next row (WS) Change to D and p 1 row,
then work 40 rows in St st.
Next row (RS) Change to E and k 1 row,
then work 40 rows in reverse St st.
Bind off.

This scarf was inspired by one of my most popular afghans. It may look complicated, but it's really a breeze to make.

FLOWERS

(make 2 in each color)

Cast on 12 sts.

Rows 1 and 2 Knit.

Row 3 Bind off 10 sts, k to end—2 sts.

Row 4 K2, then cast on 10 sts using the cable cast-on (see page 145)—12 sts.

Rep rows 1–4 seven times more— 8 flower petals.

Bind off. Sew cast-on and bind-off edges tog to form a ring.

Center flower on RS of each block and sew in place.

SIDE BORDERS

With RS facing, beg at cast-on edge, pick up and k 32 sts along first section with B, 32 sts along the next section with D, 32 sts A, 32 sts E, 32 sts C, 32 sts B, 32 sts D, 32 sts A, 32 sts E, 32 sts C. Keeping colors as established, k 3 rows.

Bind off.

With RS facing, beg at bound-off edge, pick up and k 32 sts A, 32 sts B, 32 sts D, 32 sts E, 32 sts C, 32 sts A, 32 sts B, 32 sts D, 32 sts C, 32 sts E. Keeping colors as established, k 3 rows.

Bind off.

SPOKE FRINGE

(make 1 each with E and D)

Cast on 12 sts.

Rows 1 and 2 Knit.

Row 3 Bind off 10 sts, k to end—2 sts.

Row 4 K2, then cast on 10 sts using the cable cast-on—12 sts.

Rep rows 1–4 eleven times more—12 spokes.

Sew E fringe to cast-on edge and D fringe to bound-off edge. 🖐

Winter Roses

Long after the spring flowers have disappeared, you can still wear these winter roses.

MATERIALS

- 2 1¾oz/50g balls (each approx 191yd/175m) of Rowan/Westminster Fibers, Inc. *Felted Tweed* (merino/alpaca/viscose) in #147 dragon (MC)
- 1 ball each in #155 pickle (A), #150 rage (B), #154 ginger (C), #148 sigh (D), #146 herb (E) and #157 camel (F)
- Sizes 10 (6mm) and 13 (9mm) needles
- Tapestry needle

GAUGE

10 sts and 8 rows = 4"/10cm in pattern stitch using larger needles

Both delicate *and* earthy, *these florals are brimming with charm.*

● **INTERMEDIATE**

SIZE
Approx 8" W x 64" L/20.5cm x 162.5cm

BACKGROUND
With larger needles and MC, cast on
20 sts loosely. K 4 rows.
Row 1 [P1, k1] twice, *[yo] twice, k1;
rep from * to last 4 sts, [k1, p1] twice.
Row 2 [K1, p1] twice, *k1, [k1, p1] into
double yo of previous row, then pass the
2 k sts over the p st; rep from * to last 4
sts, [p1, k1] twice.
Rep rows 1 and 2 until piece
measures 63"/160cm. K 4 rows.
Bind off loosely.

ROSES
Make 21, three in each colorway,
as foll:
1 strand each E and D, bind off with C
1 strand each B and A, bind off with D
1 strand each D and A, bind off with E
1 strand each F and C, bind off with A
1 strand each C and D, bind off with B
1 strand each B and F, bind off with E
1 strand each F and C, bind off with F

With smaller needles and 2 strands
held tog, cast on 11 sts.
Row 1 (RS) Knit.
Row 2 and all WS rows Purl.
Row 3 *Kfb; rep from * to end—22 sts.
Row 5 *Kfb; rep from * to end—44 sts.
Row 7 *Kfb; rep from * to end—88 sts.
Change to 2 strands bind-off color and
bind off knitwise.
Twist rose into a spiral and secure
with tails.

FINISHING
Lay background flat with RS facing.
Place roses evenly over background and
sew in place using tails. 🌹

Tudor Lace

The beads are already in the yarn; the lace stitch in the scarf works up easily!

MATERIALS

- 3 1¾oz/50g skeins (each approx 100yd/91m) of Artyarns *Beaded Silk* (silk/glass silver beads) in #238 lavender (A)
- 1 3¼oz/100g skein (approx 260yd/238m) of Artyarns *Silk Rhapsody Glitter* (silk/kid mohair) in #238 lavender (B)
- Size 7 (4.5mm) needles
- Stitch holder
- Spare needle for finishing

GAUGE

18 sts and 26 rows = 4"/10cm in St st with A

● **VERY EASY**

SIZE

51"/130cm L x 16½"/42cm W (across bottom edge)
5½"/14cm W (across rib)

NOTE

Scarf is worked in two halves and joined at center back.

STITCH GLOSSARY

Make Bobble (MB) [P1, k1, p1] in next st, [turn, k1, p1, k1] twice, pass the 2nd and 3rd sts over the first st.

FIRST HALF

With A, cast on 89 sts.

Preparation row (WS) [P1, k1] twice, *p5, MB, p4; rep from * to last 4 sts, [k1, p1] twice.

Row 1 [K1, p1] twice, k1, *yo, k3, SK2P, k3, yo, k1; rep from * to last 4 sts, [p1, k1] twice.

Row 2 [P1, k1] twice, p to last 4 sts, [k1, p1] twice.

Row 3 [K1, p1] twice, p1, *k1, yo, k2, SK2P, k2, yo, k1, p1; rep from * to last 4 sts, [p1, k1] twice.

Rows 4 and 6 [P1, k1] twice, k1, *p9, k1; rep from * to last 4 sts, [k1, p1] twice.

This lace-edged scarf with **glittery beads** *is perfect for making you feel so very special.*

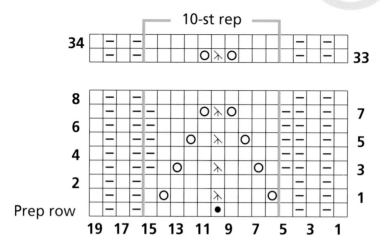

Row 5 [K1, p1] twice, p1, *k2, yo, k1, SK2P, k1, yo, k2, p1; rep from * to last 4 sts, [p1, k1] twice.

Row 7 [K1, p1] twice, p1, *k3, yo, SK2P, yo, k3, p1; rep from * to last 4 sts, [p1, k1] twice.

Row 8 [P1, k1] twice, p to last 4 sts, [k1, p1] twice.

Rows 9–32 Rep rows 1–8.

Row 33 [K1, p1] twice, k1, *k3, yo, SK2P, yo, k4; rep from * to last 4 sts, [p1, k1] twice.

Row 34 [P1, k1] twice, p to last 4 sts, [k1, p1] twice.

Rep rows 33 and 34 for 4"/10cm, ending with a WS row.

Next row (WS) K1, *k2tog; rep from * to end—45 sts.

STITCH KEY

☐	K on RS, p on WS
⊟	P on RS, k on WS
⋌	SK2P
⊙	Yo
⬤	Make bobble

Next row Purl.
Change to B and work in k1, p1 rib for 13"/33cm.
Place sts on holder.

SECOND HALF
Work same as first half.

FINISHING
Place sts of first half onto spare needle. With RS tog, join using 3-needle bind-off (see page 147). Weave in ends. ✿

Nicky says...
You can easily shorten this scarf by reducing the repeats of rows 33 and 34.

Heathered Leaf Wrap

> The leaves are sewn to both sides of the basketweave background, making it reversible.

MATERIALS

- 7 1¾oz/50g balls (each approx 97 yd/89m) of Debbie Bliss/KFI *Luxury Tweed* (merino wool/angora) in #9 blue (MC)
- 6 balls in #8 green (CC)
- Size 8 (5mm) needles
- Size 8 (5mm) double-pointed needles (2)
- Tapestry needle

GAUGE

20 sts and 26 rows = 4"/10cm in St st

● **VERY EASY**

SIZE

Approx 13" x 60"/33cm x 152cm (without fringe)

NOTE

Leaves are made separately and sewn on after scarf is knit.

BASKETWEAVE PATTERN (over 60 sts)

Row 1 (RS) [K15, p15] twice.
Row 2 [K15, p15] twice.
Rows 3–18 Rep rows 1 and 2.
Row 19 [P15, k15] twice.
Row 20 [P15, k15] twice.
Rows 21–36 Rep rows 19 and 20.
Rep rows 1–36.

SCARF

With MC, cast on 68 sts. K 2 rows.
Row 1 (RS) Work 4 sts in k1, p1 rib, work Basketweave pat over next 60 sts, work 4 sts in k1, p1 rib. Cont pats as est until 36 rows of Basketweave pat have been worked 10 times, then work rows 1–18 once more. K 2 rows. Bind off all sts.

This pattern is a **perennial favorite** *that I just had to share again due to popular demand.*

APPLIED LEAVES
(make 84)
STEM
With CC and dpn, cast on 3 sts.
Work I-cord for ¾"/2cm as foll:
K3, *do NOT turn work. Slide sts to
beg of needle and pulling yarn to
tighten, k3; rep from *. Inc 1 st each
end of last row—5 sts.
Change to straight needles.

LEAF
Row 1 (RS) K2, yo, k1, yo, k2—7 sts.
Row 2 and all WS rows Purl.
Row 3 K3, yo, k1, yo, k3—9 sts.
Row 5 K4, yo, k1, yo, k4—11 sts.
Row 7 Ssk, k7, k2tog—9 sts.
Row 9 Ssk, k5, k2tog—7 sts.
Row 11 Ssk, k3, k2tog—5 sts.
Row 13 Ssk, k1, k2tog—3 sts.
Row 15 SK2P—1 st.
Fasten off.

FINISHING
Block piece. Sew leaves onto Reverse St
st squares on front and back of scarf.
Vary direction of leaves if desired.

LEAF FRINGE
(make 18)
First leaf
With MC and dpn, cast on 3 sts.
Work I-cord for 1½"/4cm, inc 1 st each
end of last row—5 sts. Change to
straight needles and CC and work 15
rows of Leaf. Fasten off.
Second leaf
With CC, cast on 5 sts and work 15 rows
of Leaf. Fasten off. Sew to first leaf
with WS tog. Attach 9 fringes to each
end of scarf.

Moorish Medallion

Modern colors are key to this Moroccan tile-inspired scarf.

MATERIALS

- 1 7oz/200g ball (each approx 364yd/333m) of Naturally NZ/Fiber Trends *Alpine 10-ply* (pure NZ wool) each in #2002 green (A) and #2007 burgundy (B)
- Size 8 (5mm) needles
- Tapestry needle
- Fabric, 8" x 56", for lining
- Sewing needle and matching thread
- 14"/35.5cm length of purchased beaded fringe

GAUGE

17 sts and 21 rows = 4"/10cm in St st

Brocade, beads, duplicate stitch — this scarf has it all!

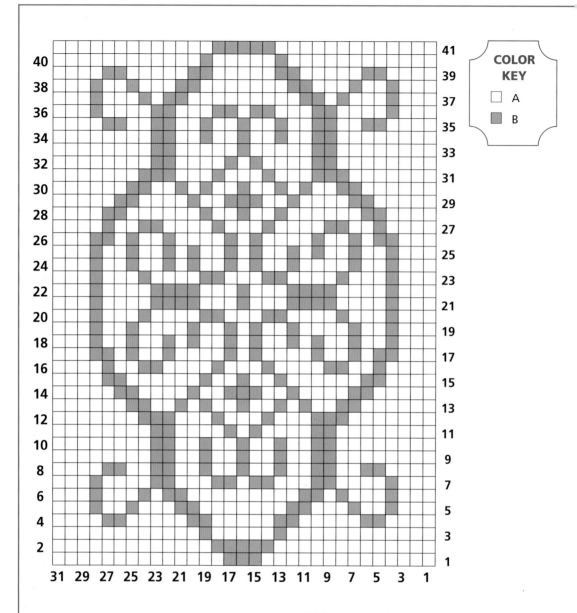

● **VERY EASY**

SIZE

7" W x 55" L/18cm x 140cm

NOTE

Scarf is worked in St st and
motif added in duplicate st.

SCARF

With A, cast on 31 sts.
Work in St st as folls:
[4 rows A, 2 rows B] twice, 288 rows A,
[2 rows B, 4 rows A] twice.
Bind off.

With B, working in duplicate st,
starting at first A row after 2nd B stripe,
work 41 rows of chart 7 times,
then row 1 once.

FINISHING

Sew lining to WS of scarf, inserting
7"/17cm of beaded fringe at each end
between woven and knit fabrics. ✿

Woven Strips

Felting can inspire you to explore different possibilities. A few simple slits in felted fabric create a fun and funky design.

MATERIALS

- 2 3oz/85g skeins (each approx 158yd/144m) of Lion Brand Yarn *Lion Wool* (wool) each in #140 rose (MC) and #132 lemongrass (CC)
- Size 10 (6mm) needles

GAUGE

14 sts and 20 rows = 4"/10cm in St st (before felting)

● **BEGINNER**

SIZE

Approx 6" W x 34" L/15cm x 86.5cm excluding fringe (Approx 10" W x 52" L/25.5cm x 197cm before felting)

BODY

With MC, cast on 36 sts and work St st for 52"/132cm. Bind off.

WEAVING FABRIC

With CC, cast on 28 sts and work St st for 65"/165cm. Bind off.

FINISHING

Felt both pieces (see page 37). Cut weaving fabric lengthwise into three 1"/2.5cm strips.

Starting 1"/2.5cm from top of body and ½"/1.25cm in from each side, *make 1"/2.5cm horizontal mark with a pencil, skip 1"/2.5cm; rep from * twice more. Cont to make marks every 1½"/4cm along entire length of body. With sharp scissors, cut the pencil-marked areas to make slits. Weave a strip in and out of each column of slits as pictured, leaving uneven lengths for fringe ties. Sew strips in place at ends of body. ✑

Think outside the box! Hot colors are felted, cut and woven for a great downtown *look.*

Basic Felting

● Place piece in a zippered pillowcase and put into washing machine. Use hot-water wash, a regular (not delicate) cycle and the lowest water level.

● Add a tablespoon of laundry detergent and an old pair of jeans for agitation.

● Check frequently, agitating until body measures correct size. Rinse in cold water, then remove from pillowcase.

● Roll piece in towels to remove most of the water. Place piece in a dry zippered pillowcase, then dry in dryer until slightly damp.

● Hand-block each piece to measurements. Let air-dry on a flat surface.

Nicky says...

If you have a knitting machine collecting dust in your closet, this would be a good time to use it to knit up the stockinette lengths you will need for this scarf.

Tea Rose

This classic houndstooth design whisks you straight uptown.

MATERIALS

- 3 2oz/55g skeins (each approx 100yd/91m) Jade Sapphire Exotic Fibres *Mongolian Cashmere 8-ply* (cashmere) in #30 la nuit (A)
- 2 skeins #50 driftwood (B)
- 1 skein each #47 blueblood red (C) and #38 wasabi (D)
- Size 7 (4.5mm) needles
- Tapestry needle

GAUGE

19 sts and 20 rows = 4" over pattern st

● **INTERMEDIATE**

SIZE
8" W x 50" L/20.5cm x 127cm

HOUNDSTOOTH PATTERN
(multiple of 4 sts)
Row 1 (RS) K1 B, *k1 A, k3 B; rep from *, end k1 A, k2 B.
Row 2 *P3 A, p1 B; rep from * to end.
Row 3 *K3 A, k1 B; rep from * to end.
Row 4 P1 B, *p1 A, p3 B; rep from *, end p1 A, p2 B.
Rep rows 1–4.

With A, cast on 40 sts.
Row 1 (RS) *K1, p1; rep from * to end.
Row 2 *P1, k1; rep from * to end.
Rows 3–6 Rep rows 1–2.
Row 7 With A, work 4 sts Seed st as est; with B, k32; with A, work 4 sts Seed st as est.
Row 8 With A, work 4 sts Seed st as est; with B, p32; with A, work 4 sts Seed st as est.
Row 9 With A, work 4 sts Seed st as est; work 32 sts in Houndstooth pat; with A, work 4 sts in Seed st as est.
Rep row 9 until scarf measures 36"/91.5cm from beg.
Divide for slit as folls:
Work 20 sts in pats as est, join two new balls of yarn, work rem 20 sts in pats as est.

Indulge! Wrap yourself in **cashmere and flowers***—you deserve it!*

Working both sides at the same time, cont in pats as est for 7"/18cm, then work across all 40 sts to join.
Rep row 9 for 6"/15cm, ending with row 4 of Houndstooth pat.
Work rows 7 and 8, then work 6 rows Seed st as est. Bind off.

FINISHING
Edging for opening
With RS facing and B, pick up and k 38 sts evenly along one edge of opening and k 4 rows. Bind off. Repeat on opposite side of opening. Overlap ends of edgings and sew in place.

SASSY FRINGE (make 2)
With A, using the single cast on (see page 144), *cast on 12 sts. Bind off 11 sts. Place rem st onto LH needle.
Rep from * until straight edge measures 8"/20.5cm. Fasten off and sew one fringe to each end of scarf.

Nicky says...
If cashmere is not in your budget, there are many beautiful, less expensive yarns you can use as substitutions.

FLOWERS (make 5)
Outer petals
With C, cast on 6 sts.
Row 1 (RS) K3, yo, k3—7 sts.
Rows 2, 4, 6, 8 and 10 Knit.
Row 3 K3, yo, k4—8 sts.
Row 5 K3, yo, k5—9 sts.
Row 7 K3, yo, k6—10 sts.
Row 9 K3, yo, k7—11 sts.
Row 11 K3, yo, k8—12 sts.
Row 12 Bind off 6 sts, k to end—6 sts.
Rep rows 1–12 four times more.
Bind off.

Inner petals
With C, cast on 4 sts.
Row 1 (RS) K2, yo, k2—5 sts.
Rows 2, 4 and 6 Knit.
Row 3 K2, yo, k3—6 sts.
Row 5 K2, yo, k4—7 sts.
Row 7 K2, yo, k5—8 sts.
Row 8 Bind off 4 sts, k to end—4 sts.
Rep rows 1–8 four times more.
Bind off.

Sew cast-on edge to bound-off edge. Weave tail in and out of eyelet, pull tightly and secure. Layer inner petals over outer petals and sew in place.

LEAVES (make 13)
With D, cast on 5 sts.
Row 1 (RS) K2, yo, k1, yo, k2—7 sts.
Rows 2, 4 and 6 Purl.
Row 3 Ssk, k3, k2tog—5 sts.
Row 5 Ssk, k1, k2tog—3 sts.
Row 7 SK2P—1 st.
Fasten off.

Sew flowers and leaves along edge of opening as pictured. 🌸

Bullets

A simple knit/purl combination creates a cool and reversible dimensional texture.

MATERIALS

- 2 3½oz/100g skeins (each approx 220yd/198m) of Cascade Yarns *Cascade 220 Heathers* (wool) in #9446 brown heather
- Size 7 (4.5mm) needles

GAUGE

18 sts and 26 rows = 4"/10cm in reverse St st (p on RS, k on WS)

● **VERY EASY**

SIZE

Approx 8½" W x 48" L/20.5cm x 122cm

STITCH PATTERNS

MULTIPLE BULLETS (multiple of 3 sts + 3)

Row 1 (RS) P3, *turn, cast on 5 sts, turn, p3; rep from * to end.

Rows 2, 4, 6, 8, 10, 12 and 14 K3, *p5, k3; rep from * to end.

Rows 3, 5, 7, 9, 11, 13 and 15 P3, *k5, p3; rep from * to end.

Row 16 K3, bind off 5 sts purlwise, k3; rep from * to end.

Row 17 Purl.

Row 18 Knit.

Rows 19–22 Knit.

SINGLE BULLETS

Row 1 (RS) P3, turn, cast on 5 sts, turn, p to last 3 sts, turn, cast on 5 sts, turn, p3.

Rows 2, 4, 6, 8, 10, 12 and 14 K3, p5, k to last 8 sts, p5, k3.

Rows 3, 5, 7, 9, 11, 13 and 15 P3, k5, purl to last 8 sts, k5, p3.

Row 16 K3, bind off 5 sts, k to last 8 sts, bind off 5 sts, k3.

Rows 17–22 Reverse St st.

SCARF

Cast on 36 sts. K 4 rows.
Work rows 1–22 of Multiple Bullet pat once, then rows 1–16 once more.
Work 6 rows in reverse St st.
Work rows 1–22 of Single Bullet pat 10 times.
Work rows 1–22 of Multiple Bullet pat once, then rows 1–16 once more.
K 4 rows. Bind off. 🧶

Something for the boys...*or their best girl!*

Oak Leaves

When autumn turns chilly, wrap up in a seasonally inspired scarf.

MATERIALS

- 2 3½oz/100g hanks (each approx 138yd/126m) of Manos Del Uruguay/ Fairmount Fibers, Ltd. *Handspun Semi Solids* (wool) in #104 multi prairie (A)
- 1 hank each in #X topaz (B), #65 wheat (C) and #V cinnamon (D)
- Size 15 (10mm) needles
- Sharp tapestry needle

GAUGES

10 sts = 4"/10cm in St st

Each leaf measures approx 3" W x 6.5" L/7.5cm x 16.5cm (after felting)

● **INTERMEDIATE**

SIZE
Approx 6" W x 72" L/15cm x 183cm

NOTE
Scarf is made in two halves. Each leaf is knit separately and felted, then sewn together in two pieces to form scarf.

LEAF
(make 41: 17 with A, 7 with B, 9 with C and 8 with D)
Cast on 5 sts.
Rows 1 and 3 (RS) Knit.
Row 2 Purl.
Row 4 Pfb, p3, pfb—7 sts.
Row 5 Kfb, k2, yo, k1, yo, k2, kfb—11 sts.
Rows 6, 8 and 10 Purl.
Row 7 K5, yo, k1, yo, k5—13 sts.
Row 9 K6, yo, k1, yo, k6—15 sts.
Row 11 Bind off 3 sts (1 st on RH needle), k3, yo, k1, yo, k 7—14 sts.
Row 12 Bind off 3 sts, p to end—11 sts.
Rows 13–18 Rep rows 7–12.
Rows 19–22 Rep rows 7–10.
Row 23 Bind off 3 sts, k to end—12 sts.

Glorious leaves are knit, felted and then stitched together to create a **showstopper.**

Row 24 Bind off 3 sts, p to end—9 sts.
Rows 25, 27 and 29 Ssk, k to last 2 sts, k2tog—3 sts after row 29.
Rows 26, 28 and 30 Purl.
Row 31 SK2P—1 st.
Fasten off.

FINISHING
Felt all leaves (see page 37).
Divide leaves into two groups as foll:
Group 1: 9 A, 3 B, 5 C, 4 D.
Place rem 20 leaves in **Group 2.**
Overlap leaves and sew in place, using photo for inspiration when layering leaves. Repeat for other half of scarf. Sew the two halves together at back neck. 🐚

Nicky says...
Making leaves is travel-friendly and also a great way to use up leftover yarn. Just make sure in advance that the yarn will felt!

Bubble Waves

A unique combo of stitch pattern, color and technique results in bubbles galore.

MATERIALS

- 1 1¾oz/50g ball (each approx 120yd/110m) of Be Sweet *Brushed Mohair* (baby mohair) each in turquoise (A) and green (B)
- Size 10 (6mm) needles
- 64 hazelnuts
- 64 small rubber bands

GAUGE

14 sts and 20 rows = 4"/10cm in pattern st

● **INTERMEDIATE**

SIZE

Approx 6" W x 58" L/15cm x 147.5cm after felting

Approx 8" W x 64" L/20.5cm x 162.5cm before felting

PATTERN STITCH

(multiple of 22 sts + 4)

Rows 1 and 3 (RS) With A, knit.

Rows 2 and 4 With A, purl.

Row 5 With B, k2, *k7, turn, sl 1 wyif, p2, turn, sl 1 wyib, k4, turn, sl 1 wyif, p6, turn, sl 1 wyib, k8, turn, sl 1 wyif, p10 turn, sl 1 wyib, k21; rep from *, end k2.

Row 6 With B, k2, *k11, p11; rep from *, end k2.

Rows 7–10 With A, rep rows 1–4.

Row 11 With B, k2, *k18, turn, sl 1 wyif, p2, turn, sl 1 wyib, k4, turn, sl 1 wyif, p6, turn, sl 1 wyib, k8, turn, sl 1 wyif, p10, turn, sl 1 wyib, k10; rep from *, end k2.

Row 12 With B, k2, *p11, k11; rep from *, end k2.

Rep rows 1–12.

SCARF

With B, cast on 52 sts. Work in St st for 4"/10cm, ending with a WS row.

Dec row (RS) *K2tog; rep from * to end—26 sts.

Note the before and after photos—both are lovely but quite different.

Next row Purl.
Change to A and work in Pattern st for 58"/147.5cm, ending with row 12. Change to B.
Inc row (RS) *Kfb; rep from * to end—52 sts.
Work in St st for 4"/10cm.
Bind off.

FINISHING
With WS facing, place 16 hazelnuts randomly over each St st end of scarf and secure each in place with rubber bands. Place a hazelnut in each B bulge and secure each in place with rubber bands.
Felt scarf (see page 37).
When scarf is completely dry, remove all rubber bands and hazelnuts. 🌰

This is how the scarf will look before it is felted.

Nicky says...
Hazelnuts were used here, but marbles, wooden balls or macadamia nuts can also be used.

Bada-Bing!

Here's a posh, playful piece that jazzes up any outfit. Have fun with it!

MATERIALS

- 3 1⅖oz/40g balls (each approx 17yd/16m) of Plymouth Yarn Company's *Foxy* (microfiber acrylic) in #21 purple
- Size 13 (9mm) needles
- Tapestry needle
- Polyester filling

GAUGE

Each ball measures approx 4"/10cm in diameter

● **VERY EASY**

SIZE

Approx 4" W x 34" L/10cm x 13.5cm

FURBALL (make 9)

Cast on 4 sts.

Row 1 *Kfb; rep from * to end—8 sts.

Rows 2, 4, 6, 8 and 10 Purl.

Row 3 Rep row 1—16 sts.

Row 5 Knit.

Row 7 *K2tog; rep from * to end—8 sts.

Row 9 *K2tog; rep from * to end—4 sts.

Row 11 Pass 2nd, 3rd and 4th sts over first st.

Fasten off, leaving a 12"/30.5cm tail.

FINISHING

Using tail, sew side seam of ball, stuffing with polyester filling before completing seam. Tie balls together in a row using tails by inserting two tail ends into the next ball and tying tightly. Weave in ends. 🍒

It's a quick and easy knit, and you'll love the way the balls connect.

Cabled Scarf With Unraveled Fringe

> The timeless appeal of cables is accented by a lighthearted embellishment.

MATERIALS
- 3 3½oz/100g skeins (each approx 103yd/93m) of Louet North America *Gems Chunky* (wool) in #58 burgundy
- Size 9 (5.5mm) needles

GAUGE
28 sts and 23 rows = 4"/10cm over chart pat

● **INTERMEDIATE**

SIZE
Approx 6" W x 49" L/15cm x 124.5cm

STITCH GLOSSARY
4-st RC Sl next 2 sts to cn and hold in *back*, k2, k2 from cn.
4-st LC Sl next 2 stc to cn and hold in *front*, k2, k2 from cn.
4-st RPC Sl next 2 sts to cn and hold in *back*, k2, p2 from cn.
4-st LPC Sl next 2 sts to cn and hold in *front*, p2, k2 from cn.

SCARF
Cast on 43 sts.
Row 1 (WS) P1, k1, p1, work 32 sts over chart pat (see page 56), p1, k1, p1, p5.
Row 2 K5, k1, p1, k1, work 32 sts over chart pat, k1, p1, k1.
Cont in pats as est, keeping 5 sts at one end in St st and working rows 1–16 of cable pat 17 times, then work rows 1–10 once more. Bind off 37 sts and fasten off 38th st. Unravel rem 5 sts on every row for fringe.

Très neat and chic!

STITCH KEY

☐ K on RS, p on WS

── P on RS, k on WS

▨▨ 4-st RC

▨▨ 4-st LC

▨▨ 4-st LPC

▨▨ 4-st RPC

8-stitch rep

15	16
13	14
11	12
9	10
7	8
5	6
3	4
1	2

23 21 19 17 15 13 11 9 7 5 3 1

Nicky says...

Five stitches are knit in stockinette stitch as you go, and then are unraveled to make a lovely fringe.

Royal Crowns

To personalize this scarf you can add initials in duplicate stitch below the crown.

MATERIALS
- 5 1¾oz/50g skeins (each approx 118yd/106m) of Classic Elite Yarns *Wool Bam Boo* (wool/bamboo) in #1603 flint
- Size 6 (4mm) needles
- Stitch holder

GAUGE
22 sts and 30 rows = 4"/10cm over St st

● **INTERMEDIATE**

SIZE
Approx 9" W x 56" L/23cm x 142cm

STITCH GLOSSARY
MB (make bobble) (K1, yo, k1, yo, k1) in next st—5 sts, turn, k5, turn, p5, turn, k1, SK2P, k1, turn, p3tog.
4-st RC Sl 2 sts to cn and hold to *back*, k2, k2 from cn.
4-st LC Sl 2 sts to cn and hold to *front*, k2, k2 from cn.
4-st RPC Sl 2 sts to cn and hold to *back*, k2, p2 from cn.
4-st LPC Sl 2 sts to cn and hold to *front*, p2, k2 from cn.

RIGHT CABLE PATTERN
(over 14 sts)
Row 1 (WS) K2, p4, k4, p2, k2.
Row 2 P2, 4-st LPC, p2, k4, p2.
Row 3 K2, p4, k2, p2, k4.
Row 4 P4, 4-st LC, 4-st LPC, p2.
Row 5 K2, p2, k2, p4, k4.
Row 6 P2, 4-st RPC, 4-st LPC, k2, p2.
Row 7 K2, p4, k4, p2, k2.
Row 8 P2, k2, p4, 4-st LC, p2.
Rep rows 1–8 for Right Cable pat.

LEFT CABLE PATTERN
(over 14 sts)
Row 1 (WS) K2, p2, k4, p4, k2.
Row 2 P2, k4, p2, 4-st RPC, p2.

Treat yourself like a princess!

Row 3 K4, p2, k2, p4, k2.
Row 4 P2, 4-st RPC, 4-st RC, p4.
Row 5 K4, p4, k2, p2, k2.
Row 6 P2, k2, 4-st RPC, 4-st LPC, p2.
Row 7 K2, p2, k4, p4, k2.
Row 8 P2, 4-st RC, p4, k2, p2.
Rep rows 1–8 for Left Cable pat.

CROWN PATTERN
(over 33 sts)
Rows 1 and 3 (WS) P9, k15, p9.
Row 2 K9, p15, k9.
Row 4 K10, [p1, k1] 6 times, p1, k10.
Rows 5 and 7 P9, [k1, p1] 7 times, k1, p9.
Row 6 K10, [MB, k1, p1, MB, p1, k1] twice, MB, k10.
Row 8 Rep row 4.
Row 9 P15, k1, p1, k1, p15.
Row 10 K8, [k2tog, yo] 3 times, k2, MB, k2, [yo, ssk] 3 times, k8.
Row 11 P7, [p2tog tbl, yo] twice, p4, k1, p1, k1, p4, [yo, p2tog] twice, p7.
Row 12 K6, [(k2tog, yo) twice, k1] twice, p1, [k1, (yo, ssk) twice] twice, k6.
Row 13 P5, [p2tog tbl, yo] twice, p15, [yo, p2tog] twice, p5.
Row 14 K4, [k2tog, yo] twice, k2, [k2tog, yo] twice, k1, yo, S2KP, yo, k1, [yo, ssk] twice, k2, [yo, ssk] twice, k4.
Row 15 P3, [p2tog tbl, yo] twice, p19, [yo, p2tog] twice, p3.
Row 16 K2, [k2tog, yo] twice, k3, [k2tog, yo] twice, k2, yo, S2KP, yo, k2, [yo, ssk] twice, k3, [yo, ssk] twice, k2.
Rows 17, 19, 21, 23 and 25 Purl.
Row 18 K3, yo, S2KP, yo, k2, [k2tog, yo] twice, k3, yo, S2KP, yo, k3, [yo, ssk] twice, k2, yo, S2KP, yo, k3.
Rows 20 K3, [yo, S2KP, yo, k3] 4 times, yo, S2KP, yo, k3.

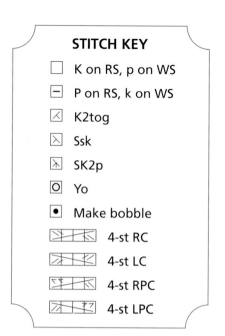

STITCH KEY

☐	K on RS, p on WS
⊟	P on RS, k on WS
⊠	K2tog
⊠	Ssk
⊠	SK2p
⊙	Yo
⊡	Make bobble
	4-st RC
	4-st LC
	4-st RPC
	4-st LPC

STITCH PATTERN

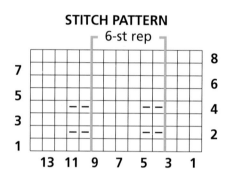

Row 22 K4, MB, k4, [yo, S2KP, yo, k3] 3 times, k1, MB, k4.
Row 24 K10, MB, k4, yo, S2KP, yo, k4, MB, k10.
Row 26 K16, MB, k16.

STITCH PATTERN
(multiple of 6 sts plus 2)
Rows 1 and 3 (WS) Purl.
Rows 2 and 4 K3, *p2, k4; rep from *, end last rep k3.
Rows 5 and 7 Purl.
Rows 6 and 8 Knit.
Rep rows 1–8 for stitch pat.

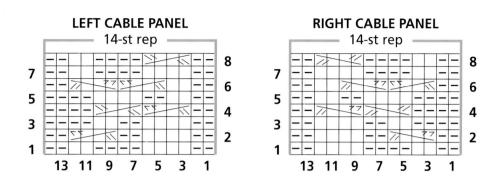

LEFT CABLE PANEL
14-st rep

RIGHT CABLE PANEL
14-st rep

CROWN PATTERN

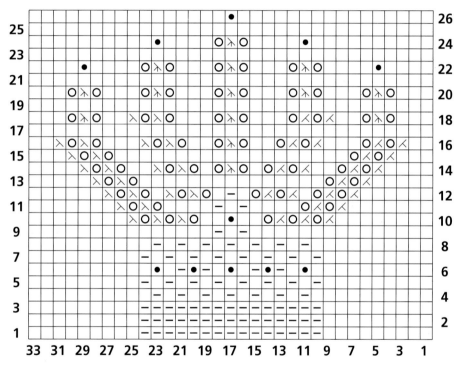

SCARF
NOTE
Scarf is worked in two halves and joined at center back.

FIRST HALF
Cast on 61 sts. K 2 rows.
Row 1 (WS) Work row 1 of Left Cable pat over first 14 sts, p33, work row 1 of Right Cable pat over last 14 sts.

Row 2 Work Right Cable pat over first 14 sts, k33, work Left Cable pat over last 14 sts.
Cont as est with first and last 14 sts in cable pats and center 33 sts in St st, work 18 rows more, ending with a RS row—piece measures approx 2½"/6.5cm.

BEG CROWN PAT

Row 1 (WS) Cont Left Cable pat over first 14 sts, work row 1 of Crown pat over center 33 sts, cont Right Cable pat over last 14 sts.

Cont as est with first and last 14 sts in cable pats and the center 33 sts in Crown pat until all 26 rows of crown pat have been worked.

BEG STITCH PAT

Row 1 (WS) Cont Left Cable pat over first 14 sts, p30, p2tog, p1, cont Right Cable pat over last 14 sts.

Row 2 Cont as est with the first and last 14 sts in cable pats, work row 2 of Stitch pat over center 32 sts.

Rep rows 3–8 of Stitch pat once, then rep rows 1–8 twenty times more—piece measures approx 28"/71cm from beg. Place sts on holder.

SECOND HALF

Work same as first half.

FINISHING

With WS tog, join both pieces using a 3-needle bind-off.

FRINGE

Cut 102 lengths of yarn 7"/18cm long. Using three strands for each fringe, attach 17 fringes evenly across each end of scarf. See page 146 for how to attach fringe. ✍

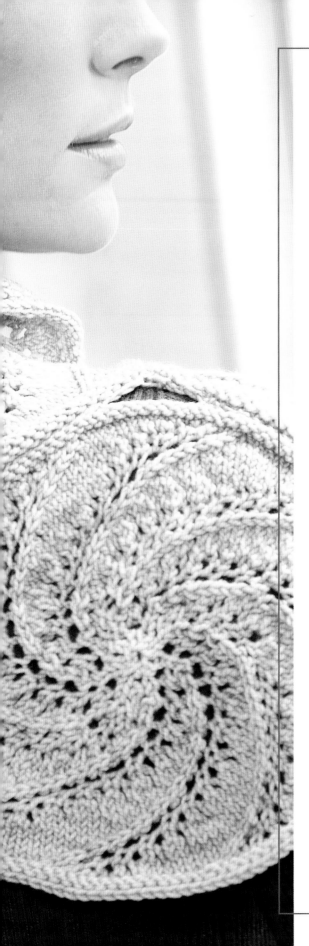

Celtic Glory

These medallions are joined together to create a fabulous scarf-wrap. You can knit individual pieces on the go and assemble them later!

MATERIALS

- 4 1¾oz/50g skeins (each approx 175yd/160m) of Koigu Wool Designs *KPM* (wool) in #2343 green
- One set (5) size 4 (3.5mm) double-pointed needles (dpns)

GAUGES

21 sts and 24 rows= 4"/10cm over St st. Each medallion measures 7"/18cm wide

● **INTERMEDIATE**

SIZE

Approx 7" W x 58" L/18cm x 147cm

SCARF

MEDALLION (make 12)
Cast on 8 sts. Divide evenly over 4 dpns. Pm and join, taking care not to twist.

Rnds 1 and 2 Knit.

Rnd 3 *Yo, k1; rep from * around—16 sts.

Rnd 4 Knit.

Rnd 5 *Yo, k1; rep from * around—32 sts.

Rnd 6 *K2, k2tog; rep from * around—24 sts.

Rnd 7 *Yo, k1, yo, k2tog: rep from * around—32 sts.

Rnd 8 Knit.

Rnd 9 *[Yo, k1] twice, yo, k2tog; rep from * around—48 sts.

Rnd 10 *K4, k2tog; rep from * around—40 sts.

Rnd 11 *[Yo, k1] 3 times, k2tog; rep from * around—56 sts.

Rnd 12 *K5, k2tog; rep from * around—48 sts.

Rnd 13 *[Yo, k1] twice, yo, k2, k2tog; rep from * around—64 sts.

Rnd 14 *K6, k2tog; rep from * around—56 sts.

Rnd 15 *[Yo, k1] twice, yo, k3, k2tog; rep from * around—72 sts.

Rnd 16 *K7, k2tog; rep from * around—64 sts.

Rnd 17 *[Yo, k1] twice, yo, k4, k2tog: rep from * around—80 sts.

Rnd 18 *K8, k2tog; rep from * around—72 sts.

Rnd 19 *[Yo, k1] twice, yo, k5, k2tog; rep from * around—88 sts.

Rnd 20 *K9, k2tog; rep from * around—80 sts.

Rnd 21 *[Yo, k1] twice, yo, k6, k2tog; rep from * around—96 sts.

Rnd 22 *K10, k2tog; rep from * around—88 sts.

Rnd 23 *[Yo, k1] twice, yo, k7, k2tog; rep from * around—104 sts.

Rnd 24 *K11, k2tog; rep from * around—96 sts.

Rnd 25 *[Yo, k1] twice, yo, k8, k2tog; rep from * around—112 sts.

Rnd 26 *K12, k2tog; rep from * around—104 sts.

Rnd 27 *[Yo, k1] twice, yo, k9, k2tog; rep from * around—120 sts.

Rnd 28 *K13, k2tog; rep from * around—112 sts.

Rnd 29 *[Yo, k1] twice, yo, k10, k2tog; rep from * around—128 sts.

Rnd 30 *K14, k2tog; rep from * around—120 sts.

Rnd 31 *[Yo, k1] twice, yo, k11, k2tog; rep from * around—136 sts.

Rnd 32 *K15, k2tog; rep from * around—128 sts.

Rnd 33 *[Yo, k1] twice, yo, k12, k2tog; rep from * around—144 sts.

Rnd 34 *K16, k2tog; rep from * around—136 sts.

Rnd 35 *[Yo, k1] twice, yo, k13, k2tog; rep from * around—152 sts.

Rnd 36 *K17, k2tog; rep from * around—144 sts.

Rnds 37–39 Purl.

Bind off knitwise.

FINISHING

Line up eight medallions and join where they meet each other (approx a 3"/7.5cm seam). Sew ninth medallion to lower edges of second and third medallions from left side. Sew three medallions tog and sew to middle of upper edge. ✥

A vintage Celtic pin adds closure to this unique scarf.

How to Create the Perfect Spiral

1 After casting on eight stitches, divide them evenly over four needles, two stitches on each needle. Place a marker, as shown, to indicate the beginning of the round.

2 Work in the pattern stitch in rounds as stated in the instructions. To work a round that begins with a yarn over, simply wrap the yarn around the RH needle, as shown, then knit the next stitch.

3 When working from one needle to the next, work the first stitch on the next needle, then pull the yarn tight, as shown, before working the second stitch. This will keep the joins neat and even.

How to Join Medallions with a Slip Stitch

1 Place the wrong sides of two medallions together on a flat surface. Insert a crochet hook under the bound-off edge on both pieces, as shown.

2 Draw the yarn through the knitting and through the loop on the hook to complete the slip stitch.

Nicky says...

We all have favorite pins—one or more can be used to hold this scarf together.

Skull-Face Mosaic

This is my favorite mosaic pattern. It depicts the head and body of a skeleton – but you have to look closely.

MATERIALS

- 3 1¾oz/50g skeins (each approx 100yd/90m) of Noro/KFI *Cash Iroha* (silk/lambswool/cashmere/nylon) in #2 ink (A)
- 2 1¾oz/50g skeins (each approx 122yd/110m) of Noro/KFI *Silk Garden* (silk/mohair/lambswool) in #246 rainbow mix (B)
- Size 8 (5mm) needles
- Size 8 (5mm) double-pointed needles (2)
- Stitch holder
- Tapestry needle

GAUGE

20 sts and 30 rows = 4"/10cm in Skull Mosaic pattern

● **INTERMEDIATE**

SIZE
8.5" W x 57" L/21.5cm x 145cm

NOTES
Scarf is worked in two halves and joined at center back. Option: To ensure the pattern has sufficient contrast, do not use darkest sections of yarn B.

SKULL MOSAIC PATTERN
(multiple of 16 sts + 3)
Row 1 (RS) With A, k1, *wyib sl 2, k1, wyib sl 1, k9, wyib sl 1, k1, wyib sl 1; rep from *, end wyib sl 1, k1.
Row 2 With A, k1, wyif sl 1, *wyif sl 1, k1, wyif sl 1, k9, wyif sl 1, k1, wyif sl 2; rep from *, end k1.
Row 3 With B, k1, *k4, [wyib sl 1, k1, wyib sl 1, k3] twice; rep from *, end k2.
Row 4 With B, k2, *[k3, wyif sl 1, k1, wyif sl 1] twice, k4; rep from *, end k1.
Row 5 With A, k1, *k7, wyib sl 3, k6; rep from *, end k2.
Row 6 With A, k2, *k6, wyif, sl 3, k7; rep from *, end k1.
Row 7 With B, k1, *[k1, wyib sl 1] twice, k2, wyib sl 1, k3, wyib sl 1, k2, wyib sl 1,k1, wyib sl 1; rep from *, end k2.

Hint: to see the whole skeleton, squinting helps!

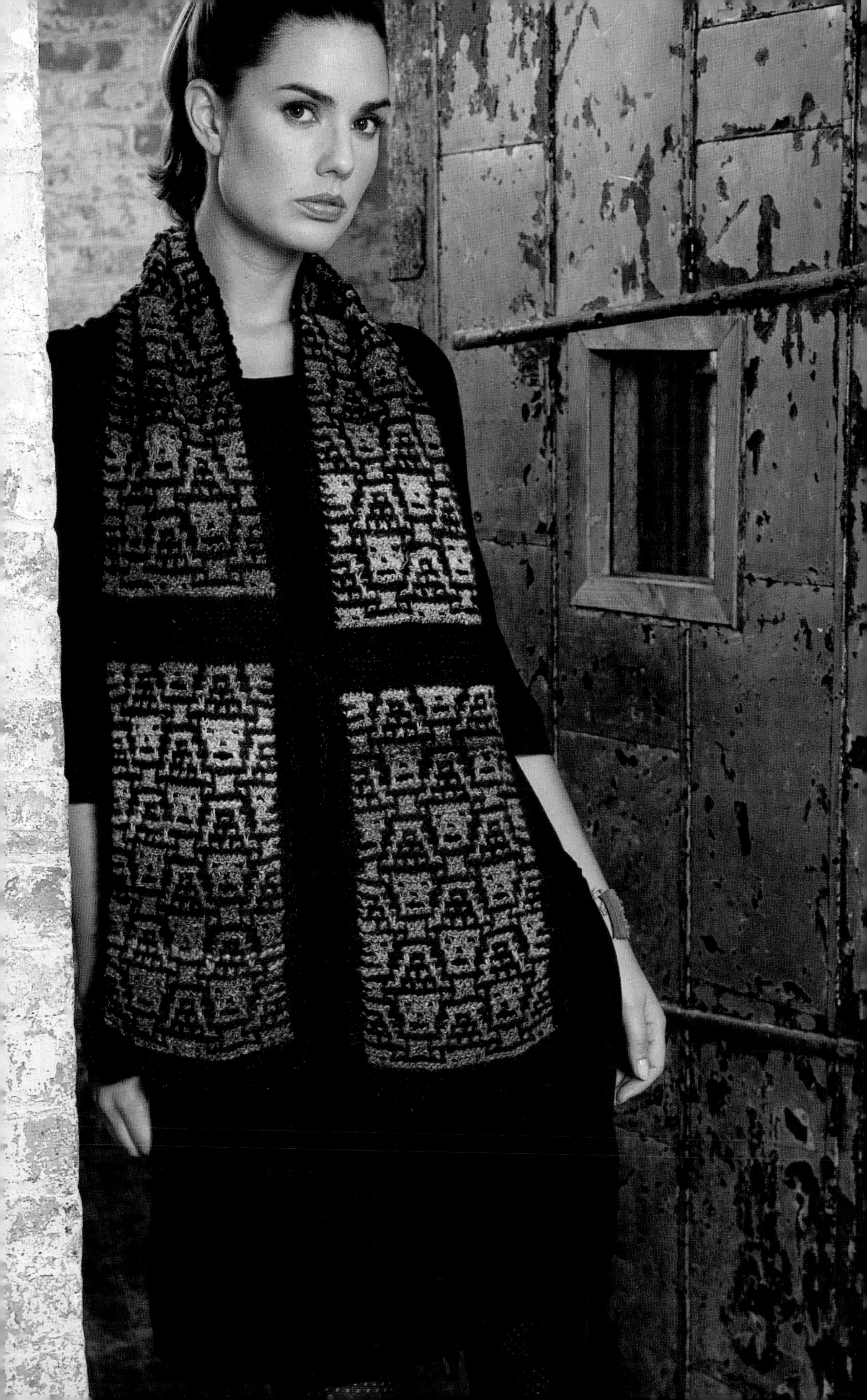

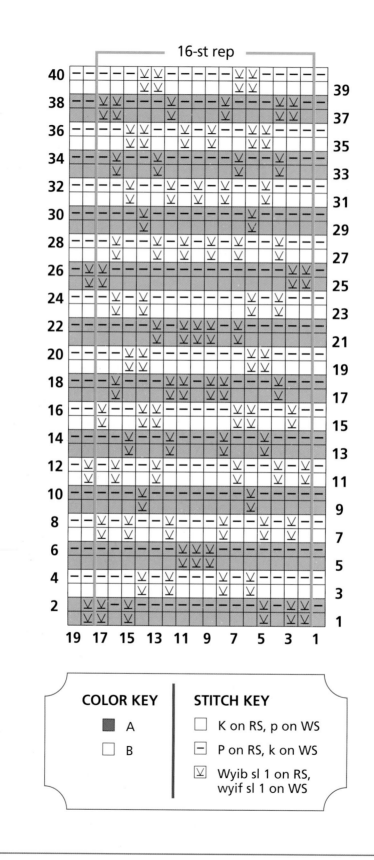

Row 8 With B, k2, *wyif sl 1, k1, wyif sl 1, k2, wyif sl 1, k3, wyif sl 1, k2, [wyif sl 1, k1] twice; rep from *, end k1.

Row 9 With A, k1, *k4, wyib sl 1, k7, wyib sl 1, k3; rep from *, end k2.

Row 10 With A, k2, *k3, wyif sl 1, k7, wyif sl 1, k4; rep from *, end k1.

Row 11 With B, k1, *wyib sl 1, k1, wyib sl 1, k2, wyib sl 1, k5, wyib sl 1, k2, wyib sl 1, k1; rep from *, end wyib sl 1, k1.

Row 12 With B, k1, wyif sl 1, *k1, wyif sl 1, k2, wyif sl 1, k5, wyif sl 1, k2, wyif sl 1, k1, wyif sl 1; rep from *, end k1.

Row 13 With A, k1, *k3, wyib sl 1, k2, wyib sl 1, k3, [wyib sl 1, k2] twice; rep from *, end k2.

Row 14 With A, k2, *[k2, wyif sl 1] twice, k3, wyif sl 1, k2, wyif sl 1, k3; rep from *, end k1.

Row 15 With B, k1, *k1, wyib sl 1, k2, wyib sl 2, k5, wyib sl 2, k2, wyib sl 1; rep from *, end k2.

Row 16 With B, k2, *wyif sl 1, k2, wyif sl 2, k5, wyif sl 2, k2, wyif sl 1, k1; rep from *, end k1.

Row 17 With A, k1, *k2, wyib sl 1, k3, wyib sl 2, k1, wyib sl 2, k3, wyib sl 1, k1; rep from *, end k2.

Row 18 With A, k2, *k1, wyif sl 1, k3, wyif sl 2, k1, wyif sl 2, k3, wyif sl 1, k2; rep from *, end k1.

Row 19 With B, k1, *k3, wyib sl 2, k7, wyib sl 2, k2; rep from *, end k2.

Row 20 With B, k2, *k2, wyif sl 2, k7, wyif sl 2, k3; rep from *, end k1.

Row 21 With A, k1, *k5, wyib sl 1, k1, wyib sl 3, k1, wyib sl 1, k4; rep from *, end k2.

Row 22 With A, k2, *k4, wyif sl 1, k1, wyif sl 3, k1, wyif sl 1, k5; rep from *, end k1.

Row 23 With B k1, *k2, wyib sl 1, k1, wyib sl 1, k7, [wyib sl 1, k1] twice; rep from *, end k2.

Row 24 With B, k2, *[k1, wyif sl 1] twice, k7, wyif sl 1, k1, wyif sl 1, k2; rep from *, end k1.

Row 25 With A, k1, *wyib sl 2, k13, wyib sl 1; rep from *, end wyib sl 1, k1.

Row 26 With A, k1, wyif sl 1, *wyif sl 1, k13, wyif sl 2; rep from *, end k1.

Row 27 With B, k1, *[k2, wyib sl 1] twice, [k1, wyib sl 1] 3 times, k2, wyib sl 1, k1; rep from *, end k2.

Row 28 With B, k2, *k1, wyif sl 1, k2, [wyif sl 1, k1] 3 times, [wyif sl 1, k2] twice; rep from *, end k1.

Row 29 With A, k1, *k4, wyib sl 1, k7, wyib sl 1, k3; rep from *, end k2.

Row 30 With A, k2, *k3, wyif sl 1, k7, wyif sl 1, k4; rep from *, end k1.

Row 31 With B, k1, *k3, wyib sl 1, k2, [wyib sl 1, k1] twice, [wyib sl 1, k2] twice; rep from *, end k2.

Row 32 With B, k2, *[k2, wyif sl 1] twice, k2, wyif sl 1, k3; rep from *, end k1.

Row 33 With A, k1, *[k2, wyib sl 1] twice, k5, wyib sl 1, k2, wyib sl 1, k1; rep from *, end k2.

Row 34 With A, k2, *k1, wyif sl 1, k2, wyif sl 1, k5, [wyif sl 1, k2] twice; rep from *, end k1.

Row 35 With B, k1, *k3, wyib sl 2, k2, wyib sl 1, k1, wyib sl 1, k2, wyib sl 2, k2; rep from *, end k2.

Row 36 With B, k2, *k2, wyif sl 2, k2, wyif sl 1, k1, wyif sl 1, k2, wyif sl 2, k3; rep from *, end k1.

Row 37 With A, k1, *k1, wyib sl 2, [k3, wyib sl 1] twice, k3, wyib sl 2; rep from *, end k2.
Row 38 With A, k2, *wyif sl 2, k3, [wyif sl 1, k3] twice, wyif sl 2, k1; rep from *, end k1.
Row 39 With B, k1, *k4, wyib sl 2, k5, wyib sl 2, k3; rep from *, end k2.
Row 40 With B, k2, *k3, wyif sl 2, k5, wyif sl 2, k4; rep from *, end k1.
Rep rows 1–40.

FIRST HALF

Garter cup edging (Beg with 7 sts and end with multiple of 14 sts)
Each cup is worked separately, then all cups are joined on the same row.
*With A, cast on 7 sts. Work in garter st for 3"/7.5cm. Cut yarn, leaving sts on needle. On same needle, rep from * twice, EXCEPT do not cut yarn after last strip—21 sts.
Joining row (RS) *K7, with RS facing k7 from cast on edge of strip; rep from* twice more—42 sts.
Next row (WS) Knit, dec 1 st at center—41 sts.

SCARF BODY

Rows 1–2 With A, knit.
Rows 3–4 K3 A, k35 B, k3 A.
Rows 5–124 K3 A, work mosaic pat over next 35 sts, k3A—3 reps of pat.
Rows 125–138 With A, knit.
Mark end of row 131.
Rows 139–272 Rep rows 5–138.
Place sts on holder.

> # Nicky says...
> Part of the charm of this scarf is the use of variegated yarn, but you will get more of a traditional mosaic look if you use two solid colors.

SECOND HALF

Work same as first half, marking beg of row 131.

FINISHING

Place sts of first half onto spare needle. With RS tog, join using 3-needle bind-off (see page 147).
I-cord ties (make 2)
With A and dpns, cast on 5 sts.
*[Do not turn, slide sts to other end of needle, bringing yarn behind sts. K5.] 4 times, [Do not turn, slide sts to other end of needle, bringing yarn behind sts. P5]. Rep from * until cord measures 8"/20.5cm. Sew one end of each tie to row 131 on each half as marked. 🐍

Yo-Yos

Yo-yos knitted and stitched together make this a unique neck accent.

MATERIALS

- 1 1¾oz/50g ball (each approx 151yd/138m) of Muench/GGH *Soft Kid* (super kid mohair/nylon/wool) each in #54 green (AA), #62 rust (AB), #28 pink (AC) and #69 maize (AD)
- 1 1¾oz/50g ball (each approx 121yd/111m) of Muench/GGH *Maxima* (wool) each in #43 green (BA), #32 pumpkin (BB), #41 fuchsia (BC) and #2 maize (BD)
- Sizes 5 (3.75mm) and 9 (5.5mm) double-pointed needles (sets of 5)

GAUGES

16 sts = 4"/10cm in St st on larger needles

Each yo-yo measures 2.5"/6.5cm in diameter

● **INTERMEDIATE**

SIZE

Approx 7½" W x 55" L/19cm x 140cm

NOTE

Each yo-yo is made up of both yarns of the same color: AA is paired with BA, AB with BB, and so on.

YO-YO

Make 60: 15 in each color, using the same color of each yarn for each yo-yo. With B and smaller dpns, cast on 14 sts. Distribute sts evenly over 4 dpns. Pm and join.

Rnd 1 (RS) Knit.
Rnd 2 Purl.
Change to same color A.
Rnd 3 Kfb around—28 sts.
Rnds 4–7 Knit.
Rnd 8 Purl.
Rnds 9–12 Knit.
Change to same color B and smaller dpns.
Rnd 13 K2tog around—14 sts.
Rnd 14 Purl.
Bind off.
Weave in ends.

FINISHING

With WS facing, position 54 yo-yos in 3 columns of 18, and 3 at each end to form points (see placement diagram). Split 12"/30.5cm lengths of B in three (two plies each) and with matching colors, stitch yo-yos together at each point where they meet. ✍

Choose the colors that make you smile!

Using this placement diagram, *you can* make the scarf *as* long or short *as you like.*

COLOR KEY
- *Soft Kid* green (AA)
- *Soft Kid* red (AB)
- *Soft Kid* pink (AC)
- *Soft Kid* maize (AD)
- *Maxima* green (BA)
- *Maxima* pumpkin (BB)
- *Maxima* fuchsia (BC)
- *Maxima* maize (BD)

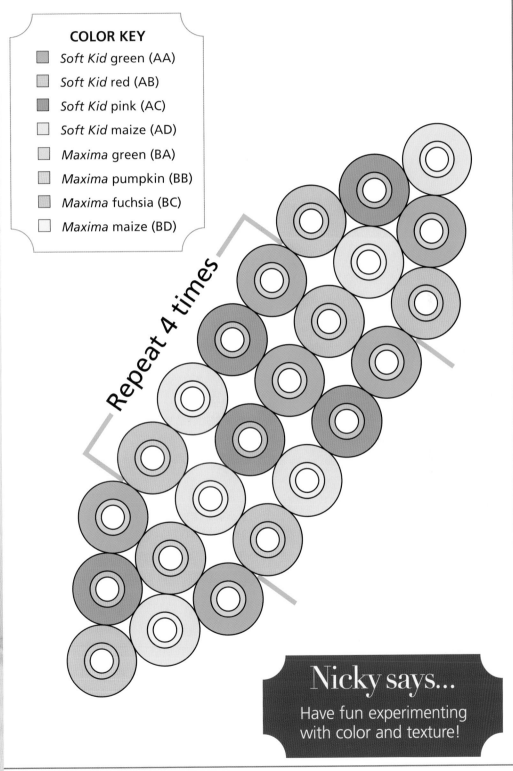

Repeat 4 times

Nicky says...
Have fun experimenting with color and texture!

Chakra

Zip up with this easy rib scarf and add your own special zipper pull.

MATERIALS

5 1⅜oz/40g balls (each approx 91yd/82m) of Diakeito *Diadrey* (mohair/wool/nylon) in #209 warm mix

- Size 7 (4.5mm) needles
- One 18"/45.5cm separating zipper
- Sewing needle and matching thread

GAUGE

27 sts and 38 rows = 4"/10cm in k3, p3 rib

● **BEGINNER**

SIZE

7" W x 60" L/18cm x 152.5cm

Cast on 57 sts.

Row 1 (RS) *K3, p3; rep from *, end k3.

Row 2 *P3, k3; rep from *, end p3. Rep rows 1–2 for 60"/152.5cm. Bind off.

FINISHING

With RS facing, mark along one edge of scarf 1"/2.5cm and 19"/48.5cm from each end. Pin zipper between marks, with bottom edge at 1"/2.5cm marks. Hand-stitch in place. ✑

Marilyn

Va va voom—
what more can I say?

MATERIALS

- 1 1¾oz/50g skein (each approx 120 yd/108m) of Be Sweet *Ribbon Ball* (mohair/ribbon/metallic) each in lemon (A), baby blue (B), eau de nil (C), pale green (D) and peach (E)
- Size 9 (5.5mm) needles
- 1¾yd purchased feather trim
- 16 yellow plastic beads
- Tapestry needle

GAUGE

16 sts and 20 rows = 4"/10cm over St st

● **BEGINNER**

SIZE

Approx 6" W x 60" L/15cm x 152.5cm

SCARF

With A, cast on 48 sts.
Work in St st and stripe pat as foll: *20 rows A, 20 rows B, 20 rows C, 20 rows D, 20 rows E; rep from * twice more.
Bind off.

FINISHING

Sew purchased trim along one length of scarf.
Embroider Lazy Daisies (see page 147) randomly over RS of scarf as foll: 5 in A, 1 in C, 5 in D and 5 in E (see photo for guide). Sew a bead to center of each daisy. ✍

Tiny embroidered daisies add an extra "wow" factor.

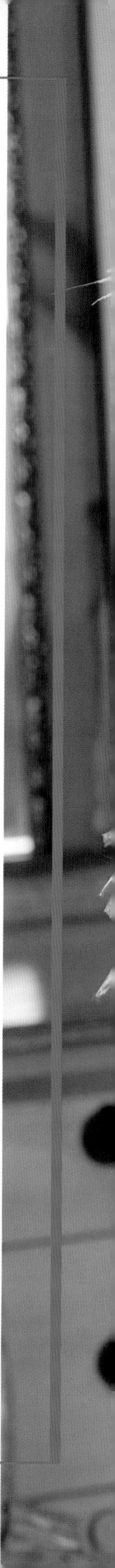

Into the Woods

> You won't find anything like this in any boutique. And making it is so rewarding!

MATERIALS

- 1 1¾oz/50g skein (each approx 125yd/114m) of Alchemy Yarns of Transformation *Sanctuary* (wool/silk) each in #30W spruce (A), #37E twig (B), #32E fig (C), #38A foxglove (D), #76E citrine (E), #35E fauna (F) and #31E olive branch (G)
- Size 5 (3.75mm) needles
- Size 5 (3.75mm) double-pointed needles (dpns)

GAUGE

21 sts and 32 rows = 4"/10cm over seed st

● **INTERMEDIATE**

SIZE

Approx 8" W x 37½" L/20.5cm x 95cm

SEED STITCH

(worked over an odd number of sts)
Row 1 K1 ,*p1, k1; rep from * to end.
Rep row 1 for seed st.

SCARF

With A, cast on 43 sts. Work in seed st for 3½"/9cm.
Change to B and work in seed st for 4"/10cm, end with a WS row.
Next row Work 15 sts in seed st with B, work 25 sts in seed st with C. Cont in seed st in colors as est for 2½"/6.5cm.
Cont in C only for 6½"/16.5cm.
Change to A and work in seed st for 11"/28cm.
Change to D and work in seed st for 4"/10cm, end with a WS row.
Next row Work 24 sts in seed st with B, work 19 sts in seed with D. Cont in seed st in colors as est for 2"/5cm.
Cont in B only for 4"/10cm. Bind off.

The leaves are easier to sew on than you think.

SMALL LEAF

(make 6 with E and 2 with F)

Cast on 5 sts.

Row 1 (RS) K2, yo, k1, yo, k2—7 sts.

Row 2 and all WS rows Purl.

Row 3 K3, yo, k1, yo, k3—9 sts.

Row 5 Ssk, k5, k2tog—7 sts.

Row 7 Ssk, k3, k2tog—5 sts.

Row 9 Ssk, k1, k2tog—3 sts.

Row 11 SK2P.

Fasten off.

LARGE LEAF

(make 12 with E and 4 with F)

Cast on 5 sts.

Row 1 (RS) K2, yo, k1, yo, k2—7 sts.

Row 2 and all WS rows Purl.

Row 3 K3, yo, k1, yo, k3—9 sts.

Row 5 K4, yo, k1, yo, k4—11 sts.

Row 7 Ssk, k7, k2tog—9 sts.

Row 9 Ssk, k5, k2tog—7 sts.

Row 11 Ssk, k3, k2tog—5 sts.

Row 13 Ssk, k1, k2tog—3 sts.

Row 15 SK2P.

Fasten off.

OAK LEAF

(make 10 with G, 7 with F, 6 with A, 6 with B and 5 with D)

Cast on 5 sts.

Row 1 (RS) Kfb, k1, yo, k1, yo, k1, kfb—9 sts.

Rows 2, 4, 6, 10, 12, 16 and 18 Purl.

Rows 3 and 9 K4, yo, k1, yo, k4—11 sts.

Rows 5 and 11 K5, yo, k1, yo, k5—13 sts.

Row 7 Bind off 3 sts, k2, yo, k1, yo, k6—12 sts.

Row 8 Bind off 3 sts, p8—9 sts.

Row 13 Bind off 3 sts, k9—10 sts.

Row 14 Bind off 3 sts, p6—7 sts.

Row 15 SKP, k3, k2tog—5 sts.

Row 17 SKP, k1, k2tog—3 sts.

Row 19 SK2P.

Fasten off.

BOBBLES

(make 19 with D, 11 with F and 7 with E)

Cast on 1 st.

Row 1 K in [front, back, front, back and front] of st—5 sts.

Rows 2 and 4 Knit.

Row 3 Purl.

Row 5 P2tog, p1, p2tog—3 sts.

Row 7 Knit.

Row 8 P3tog.

Fasten off, leaving a long tail. Sew cast-on st to bound-off st.

STEM AND OAK LEAF

(make 1 with B and 2 with G)

With B and dpns, work a 3-st I-cord (see page 146) for 13"/33cm.

Inc 2 sts on next row, then work rows 1–19 of oak leaf.

With G, work first I-cord for 3"/7.5cm and second I-cord 4½"/11.5cm.

Inc 2 sts on next row, then work rows 1–19 of oak leaf.

STEM AND LARGE LEAF

(make 3)

With G and dpns, work a 3-st I-cord to length specified. Inc 2 sts on next row, then work rows 1–15 of large leaf.

Make one I-cord (see page 146) each in lengths of 12"/30.5cm, 11"/28cm and 6"/15cm.

FINISHING

Place bobbles, leaves and stems on RS of scarf as desired. Sew in place. 🐚

Kookie-Cutter Felt

Get scissors-happy!

MATERIALS

- 4 .88oz/25g skeins (each approx 82yd/75m) of Jamieson's *Double Knitting* (pure Shetland wool) in #570 sorbet (A) and #585 plum (B)
- Size 10 (6mm) needles

GAUGE

16 sts and 20 rows = 4"/10cm over St st with 2 strands of yarn held tog (before felting)

● **BEGINNER**

SIZE

Approx 11" W x 108" L/28cm x 274cm before felting
Approx 6" W x 68" L/15cm x 172.5cm after felting

SCARF

With two strands of A held tog, cast on 44 sts. Work in St st until piece measures 54"/137cm. Change to two strands of B held tog and cont in St st for 54"/137cm more.
Bind off.

FINISHING

Felt scarf (see page 37).
Using template (page 91), cut shapes randomly over entire scarf, using photo as a rough guide.
Cut around entire edge of scarf as desired. ✿

There is no wrong way to make this, so snip away!

KOOKIE-CUTTER TEMPLATE

Nicky says...

Use very sharp, small scissors.
And don't be afraid!

Carriage Cowl

Dress up any piece in your wardrobe with this Victorian-style accent.

MATERIALS

- 2 .88oz/25g balls (each approx 122yd/112m) of Sublime/KFI *Kid Mohair* (mohair/nylon/wool) in #25 fig (A)
- 1 1¾oz/50g ball (each approx 127yd/116m) of Sublime/KFI *Cashmere Merino Silk DK* (wool/cashmere/silk) in #11 clove (B)
- Size 8 (5mm) needles
- Size 6 (4mm) double-pointed needles

GAUGE

18 sts and 26 rows = 4"/10cm in St st with A

● INTERMEDIATE

SIZE
Approx 11" W x 10" L/28cm x 25.5cm

SCARF
With B, cast on 60 sts.
Rows 1–6 Knit.
Break B and change to A.
Row 7 With A, k1, *M1, k1; rep from * to end—119 sts.
Row 8 Purl.
Rows 9–16 Work in St st. Break A and change to B.
Row 17 With B, k1, *k2tog; rep from * to end—60 sts.
Rows 18–22 Knit 5 rows. Break B and change to A.
Row 23 With A, k1, *M1, k1; rep from * to end—119 sts.
Row 24 Purl.
Rows 25–34 Work in St st.
Break A and change to B.
Row 35 With B, k1, *k2tog; rep from * to end—60 sts.
Row 36 K1, *M1, k1; rep from * to end—119 sts.
Rows 37–40 Knit 4 rows.
Break B and change to A.

The frog closures are simpler to make than they look. Just knit leaves on an I-cord and twist!

Row 41 With A, k1, *M1, k1; rep from *
to end—237 sts.
Row 42 Purl.
Rows 43–62 Work in St st.
Break A and change to B. Bind off.

FINISHING
With RS facing and B, pick up and k 52
sts along front edge. K 14 rows.
Bind off. Rep for opposite edge.

LEAF FROG CLOSURES
(make 2)
With dpn and B, cast on 3 sts.
Work four 3-st I-cords (see page 146),
two 6½"/16.5cm long for buttons and two
4½"/11.5cm long for loops, inc 2 sts on
last row—5 sts. Do not bind off.
Work as foll:

LEAF
Row 1 (RS) K2, yo, k1, yo, k2—7 sts.
Row 2 and all WS rows Purl.
Row 3 K3, yo, k1, yo, k3—9 sts.
Row 5 Ssk, k5, k2tog—7 sts.
Row 7 Ssk, k3, k2tog—5 sts.
Row 9 Ssk, k1, k2tog—3 sts.
Row 10 P3tog.
Fasten off.
Pick up and k 3 sts along cast-on edge of
I-cord, p1, M1, p1, M1, p1—5 sts, work
10 rows of leaf.
Fold shorter cord in half, twist twice to
form a button loop, pin and sew in
place (see photo). Fold longer cord in
half and twist twice, making a knot at
the fold for the button. Sew in place
opposite button loop. ✑

Classic Shibori

Nuts...oh my! This is beyond fun to make and wear.

MATERIALS

- 2 2oz/57g skeins (each approx 120yd/110m) of Lorna's Laces *Glory* (mohair blend) in #41NS china blue
- Size 10 (6mm) needles
- 150 hazelnuts or 1"/2.5cm wooden felting balls
- 150 small rubber bands

GAUGE

16 sts and 20 rows = 4"/10cm over St st (before felting)

● **BEGINNER**

SIZE

Approx 10" W x 80" L/25.5cm x 205.5cm before felting
Approx 5" W x 46" L/13cm x 117cm after felting

SCARF

Cast on 40 sts. Work in St st for 80"/205.5cm. Bind off.
Insert hazelnuts randomly on front and back of piece, securing with rubber bands.

FINISHING

Felt piece (see page 37). Let dry thoroughly. Carefully remove rubber bands, cutting with sharp scissors if necessary, and remove nuts/balls. 🐛

If you can find macadamia nuts, *use them.*

Cloud Ten

This ruched scarf has a street-smart, sassy style.

MATERIALS

● 1 8oz/228g hank (each approx 1,000yd/914m) of Cherry Tree Hill *Alpine Baby* (mohair/silk/nylon) in silver streak (A)

● 1 1¾oz/50g skein (each approx 192yd/176m) of Elsebeth Lavold/KFI *Silky Wool* (wool/silk) in #33 black (B)

● Sizes 6 (4.25mm) and 10 (6mm) needles

GAUGE

16 sts and 18 rows = 4"/10cm using A and larger needles

● **EASY**

SIZE
9" W x 48" L/23cm x 122cm

Make Bobble (MB) [P1, k1, p1] in next st, [turn, k1, p1, k1] twice, pass the 2nd and 3rd sts over the first st.

SCARF
With A and larger needles, cast on 80 sts.
**With A, work in St st for 4"/10cm, ending with a WS row.
Change to smaller needles and B.
Row 1 (RS) *K2tog; rep from * to end—40 sts.
Row 2 Knit.
Row 3 K1, MB, *k3, MB; rep from *, end k1.
Row 4 Knit.
Change to larger needles and A.
Row 5 *Kfb; rep from * to end—80 sts.
Rep from ** 9 times more.
With A, work in St st for 4"/10cm.
Bind off loosely. 🦋

New York style and bobbles *are very cool additions to this unusual* ruched scarf.

Silver Anniversary

My 25-flower tribute to *Vogue Knitting* on its silver anniversary. This also was their featured cover scarf.

MATERIALS

● 2 1¾oz/50g hanks (approx 138yd/126m) of Alchemy Yarns of Transformation *Silk Purse* (silk) in #9m pewter

● 1 hank each in #42m silver, #9c diamonda

● Size 5 (3.75mm) needles

● 25 8mm Swarovski crystals (optional)

GAUGE

24 sts and 20 rows = 4"/10cm over garter st

● **VERY EASY**

SIZE

5½" W x 26" L/14cm x 66cm

NOTE

See workshop for details on working scarf.

STAR POINTS PATTERN

Cast on 6 sts.

Row 1 (RS) K3, yo, k3—7 sts.

Row 2 and all WS rows Knit.

Row 3 K3, yo, k4—8 sts.

Row 5 K3, yo, k5—9 sts.

Row 7 K3, yo, k6—10 sts.

Row 9 K3, yo, k7—11 sts.

Row 11 K3, yo, k8—12 sts.

Row 12 Bind off 6 sts, k to end—6 sts.

Rep rows 1–12 for Star Points pat.

STAR FLOWERS

(make 11 with pewter, 7 with silver and 7 with diamonda)

Work rows 1–12 of Star Points pat five times. Bind off rem 6 sts. Sew cast-on edge to bound-off edge to form star. Weave yarn in and out of eyelet, pull tightly to cinch and secure. Sew one crystal in center of each flower.

This is a fashion statement you'll really want to make! Very chic!

SCARF BORDER

With pewter, cast on 6 sts, work in Star Points pat for 47 reps. Bind off rem 6 sts. Sew cast-on edge to bound-off edge to form circle.

FINISHING

Lay border flat in an oblong shape, with sides approx 2½"/6.5cm apart. Using photo and workshop for reference, sew flowers to edge and to each other to connect. 🧶

Silver Anniversary Workshop

1 After knitting the star-point pattern for five repeats, cut the working yarn, leaving a long tail. Thread the tail into a tapestry needle and weave it through the eyelets.

2 Secure the end of the edging to the beginning, creating a circle. Gather the points by pulling the tail tightly to close the hole, as shown above. The garter edge will pucker into the center blossom.

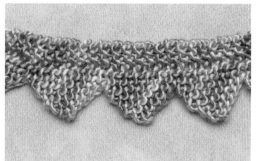

3 On wrong side, close remaining hole with tail. Weave in ends. With sewing needle and matching thread, secure crystal bead to the center of the flower, as shown above.

4 The scarf edge is created by working the same sawtooth pattern as used for the flowers, continuing the repeats to double the desired length of the scarf.

Nicky says...
Don't hesitate to use a variety of beads, yarn and colors to make yourself a truly original piece.

5 Fold edging in half and begin placing flowers in the center, alternating colors as desired. Secure flowers to each other, then to the edging, using backstitch.

Mosaic

> The back is knit in one color and sewn on – if you want to do less knitting you can line the scarf with fabric.

MATERIALS

- 3 1¾oz/50g skeins (each approx 110yd/100m) of Blue Sky Alpacas *Melange* (alpaca) in #800 cornflower (A)
- 2 skeins in #803 licorice (B)
- Size 5 (3.75mm) needles
- Tapestry needle

GAUGE

20 sts and 28 rows = 4"/10cm over St st

● **INTERMEDIATE**

SIZE
Approx 5½" W x 46" L/14cm x 117cm

MOSAIC PATTERN
(multiple of 16 sts plus 1)
Rows 1–2 With A, knit.
Row 3 (RS) With B, k1, *sl 1, k1; rep from * to end.
Row 4 and all WS rows K the knit sts and p the purl sts with the same color as the previous row and sl all sl-sts wyif.
Row 5 With A, k8, *sl 1, k15; rep from *, end sl 1, k8.
Row 7 With B, k2, *[sl 1, k1] twice, sl 1, k3; rep from *, end last rep k2.
Row 9 With A, k7,*sl 3, k13; rep from *, end sl 3, k7.
Row 11 With B, k4, *sl 1, k7; rep from *, end sl 1, k4.
Row 13 With A, k5, *sl 1, k1, sl 3, k1, sl 1, k9; rep from *, end last rep k5.
Rows 15, 17, 19, 21, 23 and 25 Rep rows 11, 9, 7, 5, 3 and 1.
Rows 26–51 Rep rows 1 to 25, reversing colors.
Row 52 With B, knit.

This **geometric** *pattern in gray and soft blue can easily be worn by a man or a woman.*

SCARF PANEL

(make 3)
Cast on 81 sts.
Work 52 rows
of Mosaic pat.
Bind off.

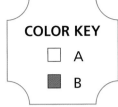
BORDER

With RS facing and B, pick up and k
28 sts along right-hand edge of any
panel. Work in garter st for 1"/2.5cm.
Bind off.
Rep for second panel.
With B, pick up and k 28 sts along
left-hand edge of center panel. Work
in garter st for 1"/2.5cm.
Bind off.
Sew panels tog, reversing color
placement of center panel.
With RS facing and B, pick up and k
28 sts along rem edge of scarf. Work
in garter st for 1"/2.5cm.
Bind off.

FACING

With A, cast on 26 sts. Work in St st
for 44"/112cm. Bind off.

FINISHING

With WS tog, sew facing to scarf
along all four edges.

STITCH KEY

☐ K on RS, p on WS

⊟ P on RS, k on WS

☑ Wyib sl 1 on RS,
   wyif sl 1 on WS

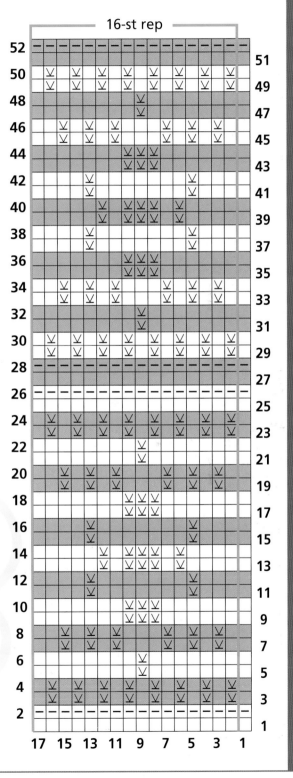

16-st rep

17 15 13 11 9 7 5 3 1

Mouse Trap

I had more name choices here than I knew what to do with. Cheesy rat? Swiss mouse? Just think of the possibilities!

MATERIALS

● 2 3½oz/100g skeins (each approx 220yd/201m) of Nashua Handknits/Westminster Fibers, Inc. *Creative Focus Worsted* (wool/alpaca) in #1933 goldenrod (MC)

● 1 ball #401 nickel (CC)

● Size 10 (6mm) needles

● Size 10 (6mm) double-pointed needles (dpns)

● 2 small black seed beads for mouse eyes

● Fiberfill

● 1 magnetic snap

GAUGE

16 sts and 20 rows= 4"/10cm over St st (before felting)

SIZE

Approx 11" W x 86" L/28cm x 218cm before felting
Approx 6" W x 54" L/15cm x 137cm after felting

STITCH GLOSSARY

S2KP Slip 2 sts tog knitwise, k1, pass the 2 slipped sts over the knit st—2 sts decreased.

SCARF

With MC, cast on 3 sts.
Next (inc) row K to last 2 sts, kfb, k1. P 1 row.
Rep inc row 42 times more—46 sts. Work even until piece measures 59"/150cm from beg.
Next (dec) row K1, k2tog, k to end. P 1 row.
Rep dec row 42 times more—3 sts.
Next row K1, k2tog, psso.

Felt scarf (see page 37).
Randomly cut "cheese holes" in center of scarf and on the edges, 1"/2.5cm, 2"/5cm and 3"/7.5cm in diameter (use photo for guide).

If this doesn't make your friends smile, *nothing will!*

MOUSE

TAIL

With CC, cast on 3 sts. *K3, do not turn, slide sts to opposite end of needle; rep from * until I-cord measures 5"/13cm. Turn and work back and forth in rows and St st as foll:

Row 1 (RS) Yo, *k1, M1; rep from * to end—7 sts. P 1 row.

Row 3 Yo, *k1, M1; rep from * to end—15 sts. P 1 row.

Row 5 Knit, inc 8 sts evenly spaced—23 sts.

Cont in St st for 3"/8cm, end with a WS row.

SHAPE HEAD

Row 1 (RS) K5, S2KP, k7, S2KP, k5—19 sts.

Row 2 and all WS rows Purl.

Row 3 K4, S2KP, k5, S2KP, k4—15 sts.

> ## Nicky says...
> Use a bold color such as red and omit the mouse, and you'll create a sophisticated geometric scarf.

Row 5 K3, S2KP, k3, S2KP, k3—11 sts.

Row 7 K2, S2KP, k1, S2KP, k2—7 sts.

Row 9 K2, S2KP, k2—5 sts.

Cut yarn leaving a long tail. Thread tail on tapestry needle and draw through rem sts. Pull tightly and secure. Sew seam, leaving opening. Stuff with fiberfill and sew closed.

EARS

(make 2)

With CC, cast on 5 sts. K 1 row, p 1 row.

Row 3 K1, S2KP, k1.

Row 4 P3tog. Fasten off.

Sew ears to side of head at first dbl dec. Felt mouse following felting instructions. Sew on beads for eyes. Attach magnetic snap at scarf neck (see photo). Attach mouse to scarf over snap. 🐭

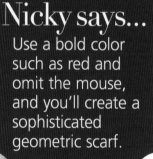

Holiday Doves

The motifs here can be worked in duplicate stitch as well as intarsia.

● **INTERMEDIATE**

SIZE
Approx 11" W x 54" L/28cm x 137cm

MATERIALS
● 5 1¾oz/50g skeins (each approx 197yd/180m) of RYC/Westminster Fibers, Inc. *Cashsoft 4-Ply* (wool/microfiber/cashmere) in #437 thunder (MC)
● 1 each in #444 amethyst, #426 mosaic, #443 kiwi, #436 fennel, #438 poppy, #441 walnut and #425 weather
● 1 .88oz/25g ball (approx 108yd/100m) of Tahki Yarns/Tahki•Stacy Charles, Inc. *Jolie* (angora/wool) in #5007 white
● 1 1.75oz/50g skein (approx 137yd/125m) of Rowan/Westminster Fibers, Inc. *Pure Wool DK* (wool) in #33 honey
● Size 6 (4mm) needles
● Stitch holder
● 2 small black beads for birds' eyes
● 13" x 45" matching lightweight fabric for lining

GAUGE
22 sts and 26 rows = 4"/10cm over St st

SCARF

NOTE
Scarf is worked in two halves and joined at center back.

RIGHT HALF
LOWER RUFFLE
With MC, cast on 120 sts. K 4 rows. Beg with a RS row and work in St st until piece measures 3"/7.5cm, end with a WS row.
Dec row (RS) K1, *k2tog; rep from *, end k1—61 sts.
Cont even in St st for 2"/5cm more, end with a WS row. Break yarn and place sts on holder.

UPPER RUFFLE
With MC, cast on 120 sts. K 4 rows. Beg with a RS row and work in St st for 2½"/6.5cm, end with a WS row.
Dec row (RS) K1, *k2tog; rep from *, end k1—61 sts.

Poinsettias and **love doves** *are sure to put you in a* **holiday mood!**

Chart 1

61 sts

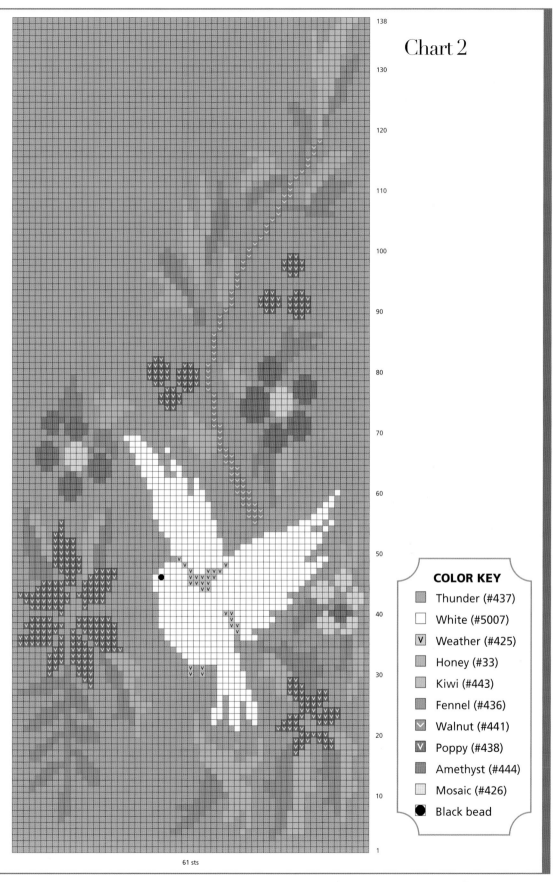

Chart 2

COLOR KEY

▨	Thunder (#437)
☐	White (#5007)
☑ V	Weather (#425)
▨	Honey (#33)
▨	Kiwi (#443)
▨	Fennel (#436)
☑	Walnut (#441)
☑ V	Poppy (#438)
▨	Amethyst (#444)
☐	Mosaic (#426)
●	Black bead

61 sts

JOIN RUFFLES

Place sts of lower ruffle onto a spare needle and position behind upper ruffle with RS facing.
*K1 from upper ruffle tog with corresponding st from lower ruffle; rep from * until all sts have been worked.
Cont in St st, foll Chart 1 for motif, until piece measures 27"/68.5cm from beg. Break yarn and place sts on holder.

LEFT HALF

Work same as right half, foll Chart 2 for motif.

FINISHING

With WS tog, join halves using 3-needle bind-off (see page 147). Sew on beads for doves' eyes. Cut fabric 12" x 45"/30.5cm x 114cm. Fold all edges ½"/1.25cm to WS and press in place. With WS together, sew lining to back of scarf. 🕊

Nicky says...

Lining a scarf is easy. After the scarf is knit (and blocked, if necessary), cut your fabric with a selvage ½" larger than the scarf on all sides, fold in the raw edge, and pin the fabric to the scarf. Sew the pieces together using a hem stitch.

Hot Wheels

This scarf came from an old afghan pattern of my grandmother's.

MATERIALS

- 12 1¾oz/50g skeins (each approx 81yd/75m) of Tahki Yarns/Tahki•Stacy Charles, Inc. *Bunny* (wool/alpaca/acrylic) in #43 light olive
- Size 9 (5.5mm) needles
- Tapestry needle

GAUGE

16 sts and 20 rows = 4"/10cm over pat st

● **INTERMEDIATE**

SIZE
Approx 9¾" W x 86" L/25cm x 218cm

LOOPY PATTERN
(multiple of 8 sts plus 7)
Row 1 (RS) K1, p2, *k1, p7; rep from *, end k1, p2, k1.
Rows 2 and 4 K3, *p1, k7; rep from *, end p1, k3.
Rows 3 and 5 Rep row 1.
Row 6 K3, *[k1, yo, k1, yo, k1, yo, k1, yo, k1, yo, k1, yo, k1, yo, k1] in next st (15 sts, including yo's), k7; rep from *, end last rep k3.
Rows 7 and 9 K1, purl to last st, k1.
Row 8 Knit.
Row 10 K4, *bind off next 13 sts, k8; rep from *, end last rep k3.
Row 11 K1, p2, *p2tog, p3, k1, p3; rep from *, end p2tog, p2, k1.
Rows 12 and 14 K7, *p1, k7; rep from * to end.
Rows 13 and 15 K1, p6, *k1, p7; rep from *, end k1, p6, k1.

Thanks, Nunny!

Row 16 K7, *[k1, yo, k1, yo, k1, yo, k1, yo, k1, yo, k1, yo, k1, yo, k1] in next st (15 sts, including yo's), k7; rep from * to end.

Rows 17 and 19 K1, purl to last st, k1.

Row 18 Knit.

Row 20 *K8, bind off the next 13 sts; rep from *, end k7.

Row 21 K1, p2, k1, p3, *p2tog, p3, k1, p3; rep from *, end p2tog, p3, k1, p2, k1.

Rep rows 2–21 for pat st.

SCARF

Cast on 39 sts. Work in loopy pat st for 86"/218cm. Bind off.

FINISHING

Fold scarf in half lengthwise with WS together. Sew side seam to form a tube. Thread a tapestry needle and run through cast-on sts. Gather tightly and secure. Rep for bound-off edge. 🦢

Nicky says...

Each ball of yarn makes seven inches of the scarf. If you want a shorter scarf, subtract one ball for every seven inches.

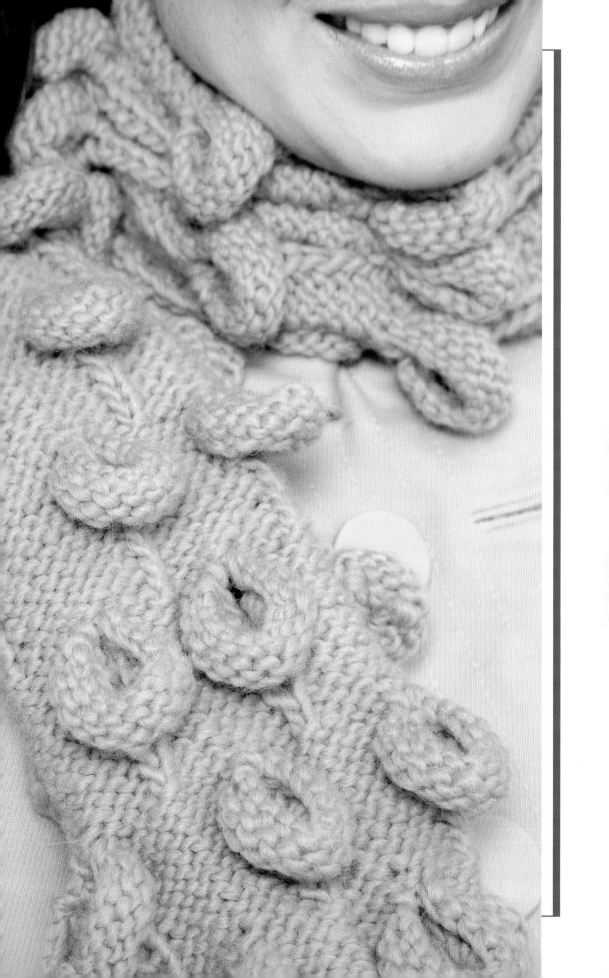

Initial Signature

> I made this scarf when I was twenty-one and it is still a staple in my wardrobe.

MATERIALS

- 2 1.4oz/40g skeins (each approx 156yd/140m) of Alchemy Yarns of Transformation *Monarch* (cashmere/silk) in #26M platinum (MC)
- 1 skein in # 37E twig (CC)
- Size 3 (3.25mm) needles

GAUGE

28 sts and 32 rows = 4"/10cm over seed st

● **VERY EASY**

SIZE

Approx 6" W x 43" L/15cm x 109cm

STITCH GLOSSARY
Seed st
Row 1 (RS) K1, *p1, k1; rep from * to end.
Rep row 1.

SCARF

Cast on 41 sts. Work in seed st for 2"/5cm.

BEG CHART

Work 12 sts in seed st, work 17 sts of chart, work 12 sts in seed st.
Cont in pats as established through row 14 of chart. Then work in seed st only until piece measures 43"/109cm from beg. Bind off. ✍

I believe no gift is better than a **personalized handmade gift** *from the heart with a kiss in every stitch.*

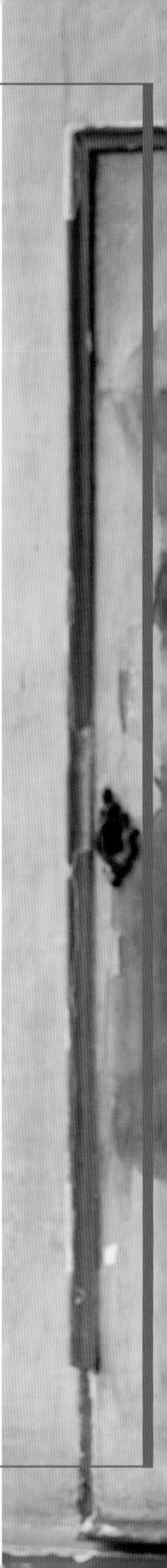

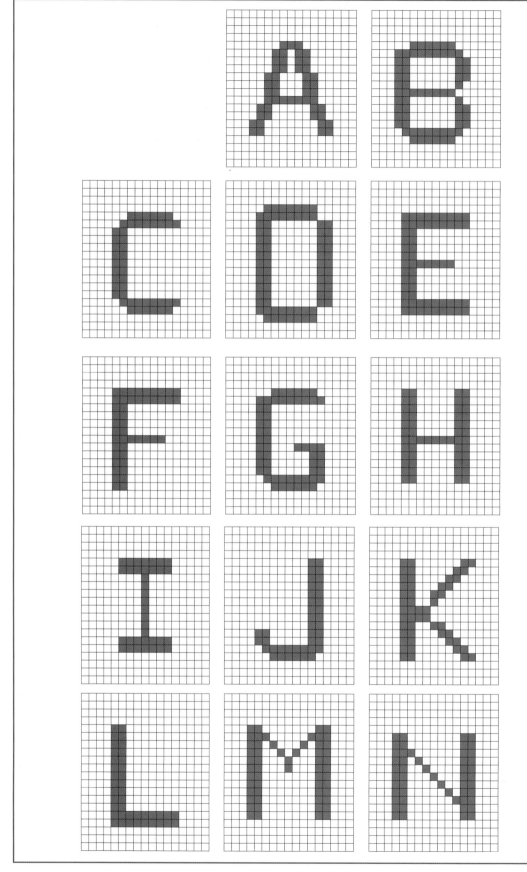

Nicky says...

You can add an edging, embroider flowers around the initial, or add appliqués to this scarf.
Use your own design skills – we all have them!

Shawl-Collar Cable Point

This is the front of one of my most popular *Vogue Knitting* cardigans turned into a scarf!

MATERIALS

- 6 1¾oz/50g balls (each approx 110yds/99m) of Schulana/Skacel Collection *Tweed-Lux* (wool/silk/cashmere) in #6 brown
- Sizes 5 (3.75mm) and 6 (4mm) needles
- Size 5 (3.75mm) double-pointed needles
- Two cable needles
- Stitch holder
- Stitch marker

GAUGE

17 sts and 26 rows = 4" in seed st on larger needles

● EXPERIENCED

SIZE

Approx 11.5" W x 58" L/29cm x 147.5cm

STITCH GLOSSARY

S2KP Sl 2 tog knitwise, k1, pass the 2 slipped sts over the k1.

3-st RPC Sl 1 st to cn and hold in back, k2, p1 from cn.

3-st LPC Sl 2 sts to cn and hold in front, p1, k2 from cn.

5-st RC Sl 2 sts to cn and hold in back, sl next st to 2nd cn and hold in front, k2, sl st from front cn to RH needle, k2 from back cn.

6-st RC Sl 3 sts to cn and hold in back, k3, k3 from cn.

6-st LC Sl 3 sts to cn and hold in front, k3, k3 from cn.

RIGHT SIDE

With smaller needles, cast on 71 sts.

Ribbing

Row 1 (RS) Work 35 sts in k1, p1 rib, S2KP (pm on this st), work 33 sts in k1, p1 rib.

Row 2 K the knit sts and p the purl sts.

You'll look great in this classic tweed Aran that's right to the point!

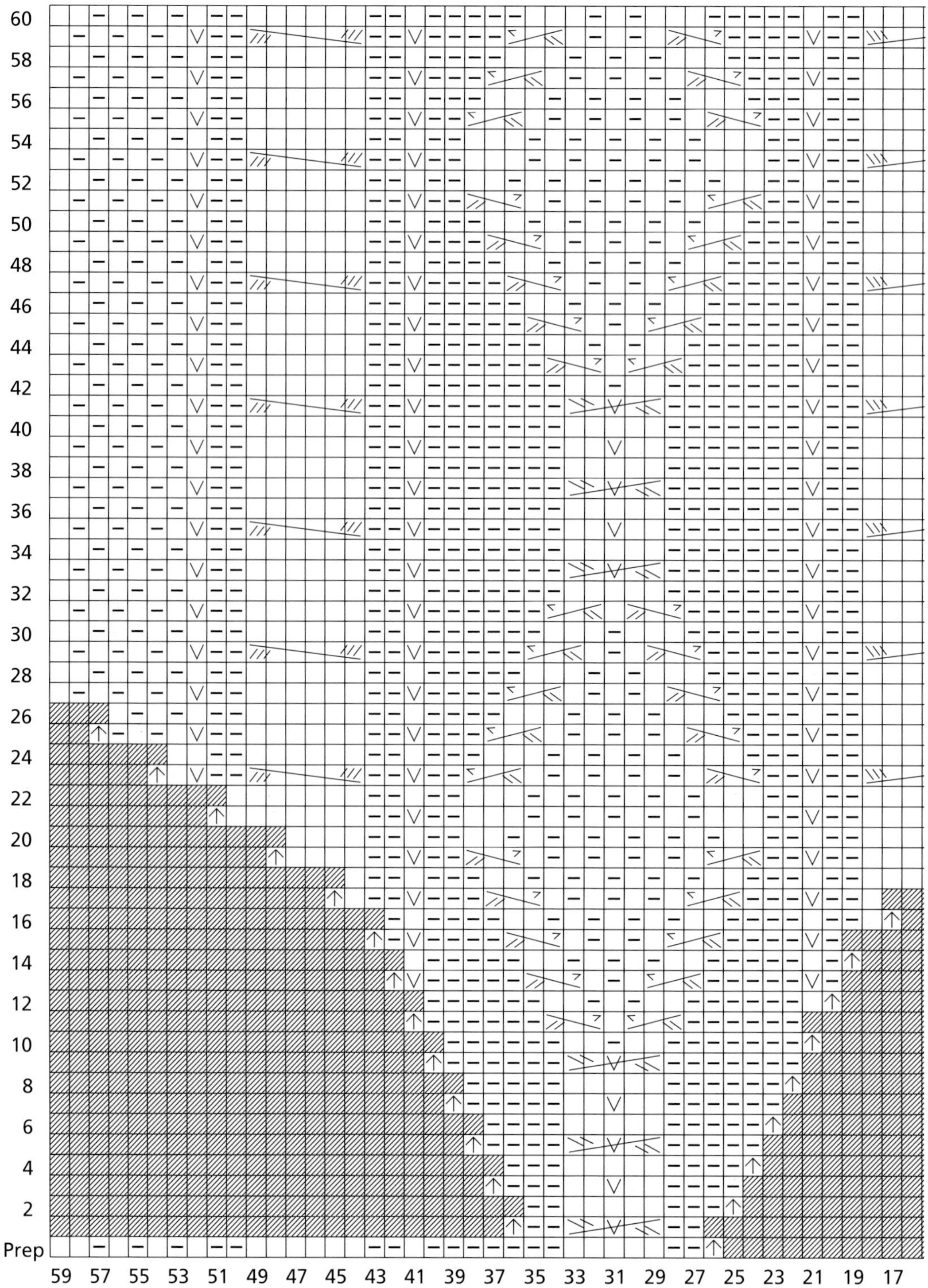

60
58
56
54
52
50
48
46
44
42
40
38
36
34
32
30
28
26
24
22
20
18
16
14
12
10
8
6
4
2
Prep
59 57 55 53 51 49 47 45 43 41 39 37 35 33 31 29 27 25 23 21 19 17

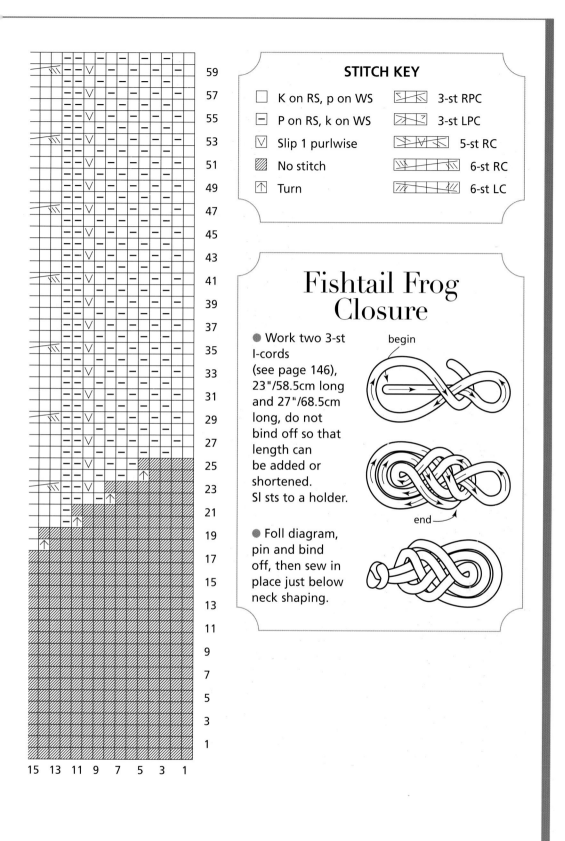

STITCH KEY

☐	K on RS, p on WS			3-st RPC
—	P on RS, k on WS			3-st LPC
⋁	Slip 1 purlwise			5-st RC
▨	No stitch			6-st RC
↑	Turn			6-st LC

Fishtail Frog Closure

● Work two 3-st I-cords (see page 146), 23"/58.5cm long and 27"/68.5cm long, do not bind off so that length can be added or shortened. Sl sts to a holder.

begin

end

● Foll diagram, pin and bind off, then sew in place just below neck shaping.

Row 3 Work in rib as est to 1 st before marked st, S2KP, work in rib as est to end.
Rep last 2 rows 3 times more, then work row 2 once. Change to larger needles and work row 3 once more—59 sts.
Beg with preparation row, work 60 rows of chart for point shaping, then rep rows 31–60 until piece measures 16"/40.5cm, ending with a WS row.
Beg dec at neck edge only as folls:
Dec 1 st at neck edge on next row and every other row 10 times total, then every 4th row 10 times—39 sts.
Work even in pats as est for 3¾"/9.5cm or to desired depth.
Place sts on holder.

LEFT SIDE
With smaller needles, cast on 71 sts.
Ribbing
Row 1 (RS) Work 35 sts in k1, p1 rib, S2KP, work 33 sts in k1, p1 rib.
Cont same as right side, reversing all shaping. Keep sts on needle.

NECKBAND
Place sts from holder onto spare needle. With WS tog, join back neck seam using 3-needle bind-off (see page 147). With WS facing and smaller needles, pick up and knit 145 sts evenly across neck edge, starting and ending at beg of neck shaping.
Row 1 (RS) K1, *p1, k1; rep from * to end.
Work short-rows as folls:
Row 2 Work in rib as est to last 4 sts. Turn.
Row 3 Sl 1, work in rib as est to last 4 sts. Turn.
Row 4 Sl 1, work in rib as est to last 8 sts. Turn.
Row 5 Sl 1, work in rib as est to last 8 sts. Turn.
Cont as est, working 4 sts less at end of next 22 rows—40 sts between last 2 turns.
Next row Sl 1, work 53 sts in rib as est. Turn.
Cont as est, working 6 sts more at end of next 14 rows, then 5 sts more at end of next 2 rows. Work in rib across entire row. Bind off. 🐚

Chain Gang

It's very festive wearing a scarf reminiscent of a paper Christmas garland!

MATERIALS

- 5 (10) 1¾oz/50g balls (each approx 87yd/80m) of Bollicine/Cascade Yarns *Revolution* (wool/nylon) in #7 burgundy
- Three size 10 (6mm) needles
- Tapestry needle

GAUGE

14 sts and 16 rows = 4"/10cm over St st

● **INTERMEDIATE**

SIZE

Small: Approx 4" W x 46" L/ 10cm x 117cm
Large: Approx 4" W x 92" L/ 10cm x 233.5cm
Shown in size Large.

SCARF
NOTE

The small scarf is made with 34 chain links (17 sets) and the large with 68 chain links (34 sets).

CHAIN LINKS

Using a provisional cast-on (see page 144), cast on 7 sts. Work in St st for 10"/25.5cm. With WS tog, join cast-on edge to bound-off edge using a 3-needle bind-off (see page 147), leaving a long tail. Rep for second chain. Using the tails, tie the two chain links tog. Sew in ends.
Make two more chain links, inserting the ends through the previous set before binding off and tying the set tog.
Cont for desired length. ✍

Memories of paper Christmas garlands inspired this long, dramatic scarf.

Il Professore

An easy 2 x 2 rib,
a fun yarn and a cool
edging make this scarf
a must-have.

MATERIALS
- 3 1¾oz/50g balls (each approx 93yd/85m) of Moda Dea/Coats & Clark *Dream* (nylon/acrylic) in #3653 teal
- Sizes 9 (5.5mm) and 10½ (6.5mm) needles
- Tapestry needle
- Small amount of fiberfill

GAUGE
42 sts in 2 x 2 rib= 7" on 10½ needles

● **VERY EASY**

SIZE
Approx 7" W x 70" L/17.8cm x 177.8cm

SCARF
With larger needles, cast on 42 sts.
Row 1 K2, p2 across row, end k2.
Row 2 P2, k2 across row, end p2.
Repeat Rows 1 and 2 until scarf measures 70".
Bind off.

BALL EDGING (make 10)
With smaller needles, Cast on 7 sts, leaving a 10" tail for sewing.
Row 1 K into front and back of every st—14 sts.
Row 2 and all WS rows Purl.
Rows 3, 5 and 7 Knit.
Row 9 K2tog across row—7 sts.
Row 10 P2tog across row, end p1—4 sts.
Pass 2nd, 3rd and 4th st over 1st st. Fasten off.

FINISHING
Using tail, sew side seam of ball, stuffing with fiberfill before completing seam. Tie five balls evenly across each end of scarf. ✍

This "smart" scarf can be tied in many ways to fit your mood.

How to Tie a Scarf

You can give any scarf the "wow" factor with these simple variations.

1

2

Classic Ascot

Easy to make, and keeps your neck extra-warm!

1 Drape scarf around neck, with right side drawn over left shoulder and again over right shoulder. Ultimately, left and right sides should hang at roughly equal lengths.

2 Use the two ends to tie a basic knot.

3 Tighten and lay one end of scarf flat over the other.

3

La Loop

A stylish shape you might see on the streets of Paris.

1 Fold scarf in half and lay across shoulders with scarf crease on one side and scarf ends on the other.

2 Tuck both ends of scarf through the loop created by the crease.

3 Tighten.

Twist & Shout

Here's a variation on La Loop.

1 Fold scarf in half and twist. Lay scarf across shoulders with scarf crease on one side and scarf ends on the other.

2 Tuck both ends of scarf through the loop created by the crease.

Big Bow

Simple, adorable, irresistible!

1 Drape scarf around neck with left and right sides hanging at roughly equal lengths.

2 Make a basic knot.

3 Make a simple bow.

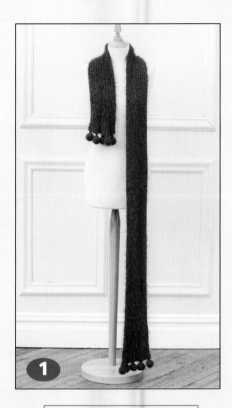

Wonder Weave

It's easier than it looks!

1 Drape scarf around neck with left side hanging much lower than right side.

2 Bring left side across front, drape over right shoulder and again over left shoulder.

3 Tuck left end under right end and through loop.

4 Pull tight to secure.

Scarf Edgings

Ta-dah! Here are ten of my favorite edgings that can be added to any scarf for extra pizzazz. You can be the designer!

1. GARTER CUPS
(beg with 7 sts and end with multiple of 14 sts)
● Each cup is worked separately, then all cups are joined on the same row.
● Cut yarn on all but last cup and leave sts on needle.
Cast on 7 sts.
Work in garter st for 3"/7.5cm.
Cut yarn and leave sts on needle.
On same needle, cast on and work as before to make another strip. Cont in this manner until desired number of strips are made (each strip makes 14 sts).
To join cups:
*K7, with RS facing, k7 from cast on edge; rep from * to last strip. Cont as desired. ✍

2. KNOTTED FLAP
(multiple of 10 sts)
● Each flap is worked separately, then all flaps are joined on the same row.
● Break yarn on all but last flap and leave sts on needle.
Work from ** to ** of Button Flap as foll:
Cast on 9 sts.
Row 1 *K1, p1; rep from *, end k1.
Rep Row 1 for 4"/10cm.
Break yarn and leave sts on needle. On same needle, cast on and work as above to make another flap. Cont in this manner until desired number of flaps are made.
To join flaps, *work 9 sts from 1 flap on LH needle, cast on 1 st; rep from * to last flap, k9.
Cont in seed st or as desired.
Knot ends of each or alternating flap, as desired. ✍

3. HOOK LOOPS
(beg with 8 sts and end with multiple of 16 sts)
● Each loop is worked separately, then all loops are joined on the same row.
● Cut yarn on all but last strip and leave sts on needle.
● Alternate colors as desired.
Cast on 8 sts.
Work in St st for 4"/10cm.
Cut yarn and leave sts on needle.
On same needle, cast on and work as before to make another strip. Cont in this manner until desired number of strips are made (each strip makes 16 sts).
To join links:
*K8, bring cast on edge of first strip behind second strip. Using 3-needle joining technique (see page 188), k8 from second strip tog with 8 sts picked up from cast-on edge; rep from * to last strip, k8 from cast-on edge of last strip.
Purl 1 row.
Cont as desired. ✍

4. MOCK TASSEL RIB
(multiple of 7 sts plus 2)
Row 1 (RS) P2, *k1 tbl, [p1, k1 tbl] twice, p2; rep from * to end.
Row 2 K2, *p1 tbl, [k1, p1 tbl] twice, k2; rep from * to end.
Rep rows 1 and 2 for 2"/5cm, end with a WS row.
Row 3 P2, *sl next 5 sts to cn and wrap yarn counterclockwise around cn (snugly) 4 times, sl these 5 sts onto RH needle, p2; rep from * to end.
Row 4 K2, *p5, k2; rep from * to end.
Row 5 P2, *k5, p2; rep from * to end.
Row 6 K2, *1/1 RPC, p1, 1/1 LPC, k2; rep

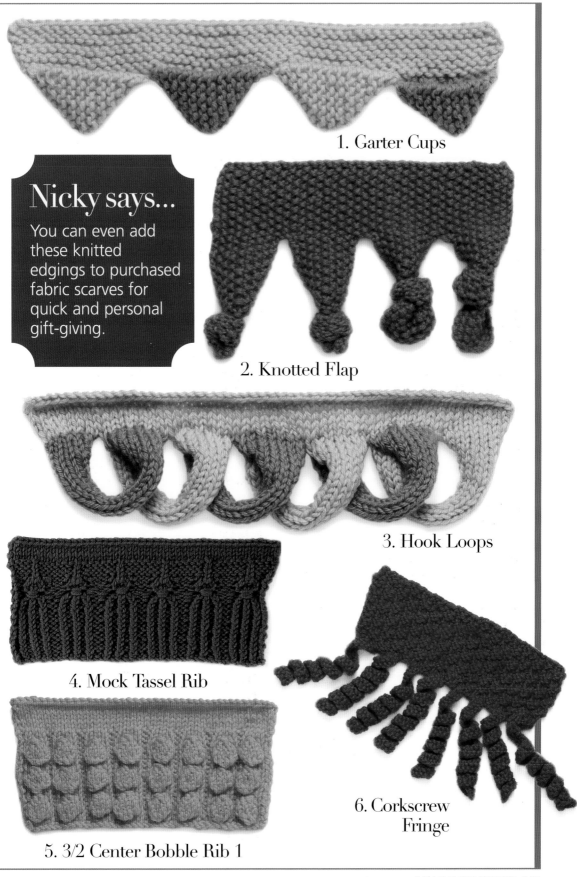

1. Garter Cups

Nicky says...

You can even add these knitted edgings to purchased fabric scarves for quick and personal gift-giving.

2. Knotted Flap

3. Hook Loops

4. Mock Tassel Rib

6. Corkscrew Fringe

5. 3/2 Center Bobble Rib 1

from * to end.
Row 7 P3, *M1, s2kp, M1, p4; rep from *, end last rep p3.
Row 8 K4, *p1, k6; rep from *, end last rep k4.
Row 9 P4, *k1, p6; rep from *, end last rep p4.
Row 10 Rep row 8.
Cont as desired. 🐏

5. 3/2 CENTER BOBBLE RIB I
(multiple of 5 sts plus 2)
Make bobble (MB) [(K1, p1]) twice, k1] into same st—5 sts; turn, p5, turn, k5, turn, p5, turn; pass 2nd, 3rd, 4th and 5th sts, one at a time, over first st, sl st back to RH needle.
Rows 1 and 3 (RS) P2, *k3, p2; rep from * to end.
Rows 2, 4 and 6 K2, *p3, k2; rep from * to end.
Row 5 P2, *k1, MB, k1, p2; rep from * to end.
Rep rows 1 to 6 until desired length, end with row 2.
Cont as desired. 🐏

6. CORKSCREW FRINGE
(Cast on over two needles or very loosely—any number of sts)
● The fringe is knitted separately and then attached. The yarn weight and number of sts cast on will determine the length. Loosely cast on any number of sts.
Row 1 K into the front, back and front again of each st across.
Row 2 Bind off purlwise. Use fingers to twist each tassel into a corkscrew. 🐏

7. CORD FRINGE (attached)
Make desired number of cords of any size and color. Bind off sts when cord is desired length, leaving a 4"/10cm tail. Attach each cord to an edge by pulling tail through to back of work and tying it at back of piece.
Cords can also be layered by pulling the tails through sts in middle of fabric. 🐏

8. KING'S BALL
Cast on 10 sts, leaving a long tail for seaming.
Row 1 K into front and back of every st—20 sts.
Row 2 and all WS rows Purl.
Rows 3, 5, 7, 9 and 11 Knit.
Row 13 *K2tog; rep from * to end—10 sts.
Row 14 *P2tog; rep from * to end—5 sts.
With dpn work St st cord For desired length. Place on holder. Cont in this manner until desired number of balls are made, alternating lengths of cords as desired.
With tapestry needle, run thread through cast-on sts and gather, securing thread. Stuff with polyfill. Sew side edges together.
To join balls:
*K5 cord sts, turn, cast on 5 sts, turn; rep from * to end.
Cont as desired. 🐏

9. CURLY CUE TRIM
Cast on number of sts needed for edge. On spare needle, work corkscrew fringe (see above) long enough to fit along edge. With spare needle, pick up st on each twist. With both needles parallel, *k corkscrew and cast-on st tog, k3 cast-on sts; rep from *, end k corkscrew and cast-on st tog.
Cont as desired. 🐏

10. FRISEUR FRINGE
Cast on 23 sts.
Rows 1, 2, 5 and 6 Knit.
Rows 3 and 7 Bind off 19 sts, k to end—4 sts.
Row 4 K4, using the cable cast-on method, cast on 19 sts.
Rep rows 4 to 7 until desired length, end with row 6. Bind off. 🐏

Edgings make the simplest scarves "wow" pieces!

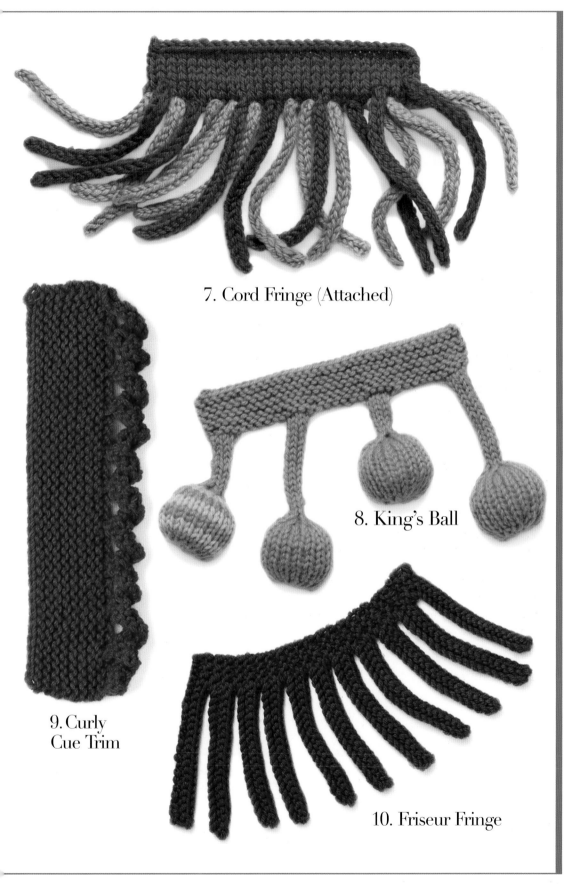

7. Cord Fringe (Attached)

8. King's Ball

9. Curly Cue Trim

10. Friseur Fringe

Techniques

Single Cast-On

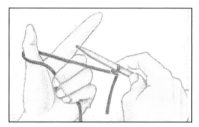

1 Place a slip knot on the right needle, leaving a short tail. Wrap the yarn from the ball around your left thumb from front to back and secure it in your palm with your other fingers.

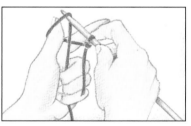

2 Insert the needle upward through the strand on your thumb.

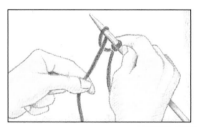

3 Slip this loop from your thumb onto the needle, pulling the yarn from the ball to tighten it. Continue in this way until all the stitches are cast on.

Provisional Cast-On

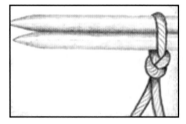

1 This is a cast-on method used when stitches are to be picked up and worked later, such as for hems or special edges. Using two needles held together, begin with a slipknot.

2 Hold a long strand of waste yarn beside the slipknot and take the working yarn under the waste yarn and then behind it again until all stitches are cast on.

3 Before knitting, withdraw one needle, then knit into the front of the loops on the first row. Leave waste yarn in until you are ready to pick up stitches and add your edge later.

Cable Cast-On

1 Cast on two stitches using the knitting-on cast-on described on page 5. *Insert the right needle between the two stitches on the left needle.

2 Wrap the yarn around the right needle as if to knit and pull the yarn through to make a new stitch.

3 Place the new stitch on the left needle as shown. Repeat from the *, always inserting the right needle in between the last two stitches on the left needle.

Abbreviations

Beg = begin / beginning

CC = contrasting color

Ch = chain

Cn = cable needle

Cont = continue

Dec = decrease

Dpn = double pointed needles

Est = established

Foll = follows / following

K = knit

K2tog = knit 2 sts together

Kfb = knit into the front & back of next st

M1 = make 1 (increase)

MC = main color

P = purl

P2tog = purl 2 sts together

Pat = pattern

Pfb = purl into the front & back of next st

Pm = place marker

Psso = pass slipped st over

Rem = remain / remaining

Rep = repeat

RS = right side

Sc = single crochet

SKP = slip 1 st, k1 st, pass sl st over k st

SK2P = slip 1 st, k2tog, pass sl st over k2tog

Ssk = slip, slip, knit

Sl = slip

St = stitch

Tbl = through back loop

Tog = together

WS = wrong side

Wyib = with yarn in back

Wyif = with yarn in front

Yo = yarn over

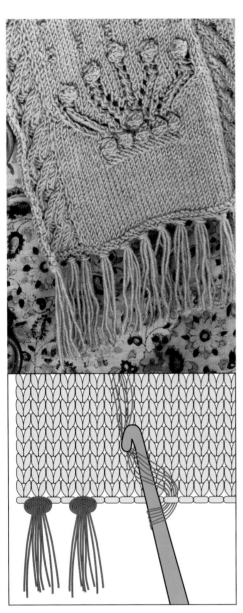

Simple Fringe

Cut yarn twice desired length plus extra
for knotting. On wrong side, insert
hook from front to back through piece
and over folded yarn. Pull yarn through.
Draw ends through and tighten.
Trim yarn.

Knit I-Cord

Using dpns or a short circular
needle, cast on 3 sts or the number
of stitches required.

ROW 1 K3, do not turn, slide sts to
other end of needle. Rep row 1 to
desired length. Bind off.

Three-Needle Bind-Off

This bind-off is used to join two edges that have the same number of stitches, which have been placed on holders.

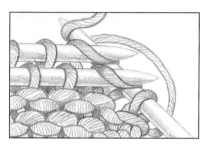

1 With the right side of the two pieces facing each other, and the needles parallel, insert a third needle knitwise into the first stitch of each needle. Wrap the yarn around the needle as if to knit.

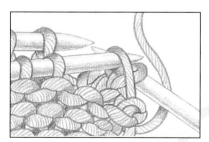

2 Knit these two stitches together and slip them off the needles. *Knit the next two stitches together in the same way as shown.

3 Slip the first stitch on the third needle over the second stitch and off the needle. Repeat from the * in step 2 across the row until all the stitches are bound off.

Duplicate Stitch

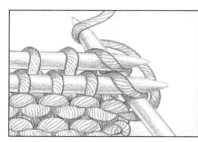

1

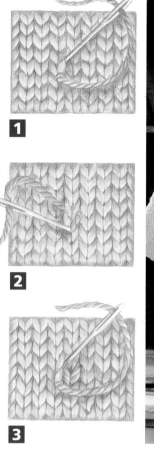

2

3

Lazy Daisy Stitch

Three-Needle Joining Technique

Work steps 1–2 of Three-needle bind-off.

Many thanks to my dedicated, talented knitters:

Clare Brenner, Eileen Curry, Tanis Gray, Nancy Henderson, Maggie MacManus, Dianne Weitzul and Eve Wilkin

Also thanks to:
● Marcus Tullis (who shot my first book, *The Knit Hat Book!*) and Jenny Acheson, Jack Deutsch, and Rose Callahan for the lovely photography that brought the scarves to life.

● My steadfast fans and family for their support and advice:

Jo Brandon, Nora Kravis, Chris Kitch, Jenni Stone, Leigh Merryfield, Aunt Angie, Anne Brenner, Nancy Henderson, Jeanine Johnson, Samantha Dornfeld and Ben Quinones

● The hardworking SoHo staff: Trisha Malcolm, Adina Klein, Tanis Gray, Carla Scott, Elaine Silverstein, Diane Lamphron, Erica Smith and Sheena T. Paul

● Instructions editors Charlotte Parry and Eve Ng

● The many yarn companies for their generosity and the speed with which they got their beautiful yarns to me, and to Andrea Waller of Seaport Yarn, New York

And a special thank-you to my beautiful niece, Tristan Quinones, for her help in coming up with a name for this book!

Also, to Howard—you rock!

Photo Credits

Jenny Acheson
Back cover,
pages 11, 13, 18, 21, 23, 25, 30, 31, 33, 35, 45, 47, 52, 64, 67, 71, 74, 80, 81, 83, 85, 87, 89, 90, 96, 100, 108, 111, 112, 117, 119, 121, 126, 131

Rose Callahan
Front cover,
pages 9, 38, 41, 54, 57, 77, 78, 133

Jack Deutsch
pages 8, 97, 109, 110, 135, 136–139, 141, 143

Marcus Tullis
pages 15, 17, 27, 29, 42, 49, 50, 51, 59, 63, 68, 69, 92, 95, 98, 102, 103, 105, 106, 123, 136–139, 148

SPECIAL THANKS
to Urban Outfitters for wardrobe and accessories.

Resources

**Alchemy Yarns
of Transformation**
P.O. Box 1080
Sebastopol, CA 95473
www.alchemyyarns.com

Artyarns
39 Westmoreland Avenue
White Plains, NY 10606
www.artyarns.com

Be Sweet
1315 Bridgeway
Sausalito, CA 94965
www.besweetproducts.com

Bollicine
Distributed by Cascade Yarns

Blue Sky Alpacas
P.O. Box 88
Cedar, MN 55011
www.blueskyalpacas.com

Cascade Yarns
1224 Andover Park East
Tukwila, WA 98188
www.cascadeyarns.com

Cherry Tree Hill
100 Cherry Tree Hill Lane
Barton, VT 05822
www.cherryyarn.com

Classic Elite Yarns
122 Western Avenue
Lowell, MA 01851
www.classiceliteyarns.com

Coats & Clark
P.O. Box 12229
Greenville, SC 29612
www.coatsandclark.com

Dancing Fibers
7018 82nd Street #9
Lubbock, TX 79424
www.dancingfibers.com

Debbie Bliss
Distributed by KFI

Diakeito
Distributed by Dancing
Fibers

Elsebeth Lavold
Distributed by KFI

Fairmount Fibers, Ltd.
915 North 28th Street
Philadelphia, PA 19130
www.fairmountfibers.com

Fiber Trends
P.O. Box 7266
E. Wenatchee, WA 98802
www.fibertrends.com

GGH
Distributed by
Muench Yarns

**Jade Sapphire
Exotic Fibres**
866.857.3897
www.jadesapphire.com

Knitting Fever, Inc.
P.O. Box 336
315 Bayview Avenue
Amityville, NY 11701
www.knittingfever.com

Koigu Wool Designs
Box 158
563295 Glenelg Holland
Townline
Chatsworth, Ontario
N0H 1G0
Canada
www.koigu.com

Lion Brand Yarn
34 West 15th Street
New York, NY 10011
www.lionbrand.com

Lorna's Laces
4229 North Honore Street
Chicago, IL 60613
www.lornaslaces.net

Louet North America
808 Commerce Park Drive
Ogdensburg, NY 13669
In Canada:
R.R. 4
Prescott, Ontario K0E 1T0
Canada
www.louet.com

Manos del Uruguay
Distributed by
Fairmount Fibers, Ltd.
www.manos.com/uy

Moda Dea
Distributed by
Coats & Clark
www.modadea.com

Muench Yarns, Inc.
1323 Scott Street
Petaluma, CA 94954-1135
www.myyarn.com

Nashua Handknits
Distributed by
Westminster Fibers, Inc.

Naturally NZ
15 Church Street
Onehunga
Auckland, New Zealand
www.naturallyyarnsnz.com
In the USA: Distributed by
Fiber Trends
In Canada: Distributed by
The Old Mill Knitting Co.

Noro
Distributed by KFI

**The Old Mill
Knitting Co.**
P.O. Box 81176
Ancaster, Ontario L9G 4X2
Canada
www.oldmillknitting.com

Plymouth Yarn Co.
P.O. Box 28
Bristol, PA 19007
www.plymouthyarn.com

Rowan
Distributed by
Westminster Fibers, Inc.
www.knitrowan.com
In the U.K.: Green Lane Mill
Holmfirth
HD9 2DX England
www.knitrowan.com

RYC
Distributed by
Westminster Fibers, Inc.

Schulana
Distributed by Skacel
Collection, Inc.

Skacel Collection, Inc.
8041 South 180th Street
Kent, WA 98032
www.skacelknitting.com

Sublime
Distributed by KFI

Tahki•Stacy Charles, Inc.
70-30 80th Street,
Building 36
Ridgewood, NY 11385
www.tahkistacycharles.com

Tahki Yarns
Distributed by Tahki•Stacy
Charles, Inc.

Westminster Fibers
4 Townsend Avenue,
Unit 8
Nashua, NH 03063
www.westminsterfibers.com

Index

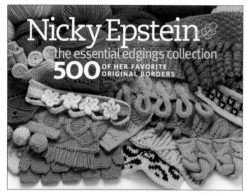

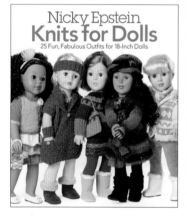
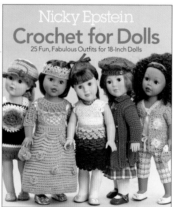

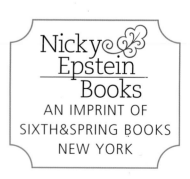